T0094948

BOB MARLEY, MY SON

BOB MARLEY, MY SON

Cedella Marley Booker
with Anthony C. Winkler

TAYLOR TRADE PUBLISHING
Lanham • Boulder • New York • London

First Taylor Trade Publishing edition 2003

This Taylor Trade Publishing paperback edition of *Bob Marley, My Son* is an unabridged republication of the hardcover edition (originally titled *Bob Marley: An Intimate Portrait by His Mother*) first published in the United Kingdom in 1996. It is reprinted by arrangement with the authors.

Published by Taylor Trade Publishing
An imprint of The Rowman & Littlefield Publishing Group, Inc.
4501 Forbes Boulevard, Suite 200, Lanham, Maryland 20706
www.rowman.com

Unit A, Whitacre Mews, 26-34 Stannary Street, London SE11 4AB, United Kingdom

Distributed by NATIONAL BOOK NETWORK

Copyright © 1996 by Cedella Marley Booker and Anthony C. Winkler
First paperback edition 2015

All rights reserved. No part of this book may be reproduced in any form or by any electronic or mechanical means, including information storage and retrieval systems, without written permission from the publisher, except by a reviewer who may quote passages in a review.

British Library Cataloguing in Publication Information Available

Library of Congress Cataloging-in-Publication Data
The hardback edition of this book was previously catalogued by the Library of Congress as follows:

Booker, Cedella Marley.
     Bob Marley, my son / Cedella Marley Booker with Anthony C. Winkler.
          p. cm.
     Includes index.
     Originally published: London : Viking, 1996.
     1. Marley, Bob. 2. Reggae musicians–Jamaica–Biography. I. Winkler, Anthony C. II. Title.

ML420.M3313 B65 2003
782.421646'092–dc21   2003040181

ISBN 0-87833-298-7 (cloth : alk. paper)
ISBN 978-1-63076-077-9 (pbk. : alk. paper)

♾™ The paper used in this publication meets the minimum requirements of American National Standard for Information Sciences—Permanence of Paper for Printed Library Materials, ANSI/NISO Z39.48-1992.

Chapter One

My life, like every life, has been a chain of separate moments – some wonderful, many ordinary, a few terrible. A terrible moment in my life arrived one evening in the summer of 1977 with an unexpected telephone call from Bob Marley, my son.

I was in Wilmington, Delaware, cooking dinner, when the phone rang. It was Bob, calling from England. His voice sounded shaky. He had just taken a medical test and the results, he said, showed that he had cancer in his big toe.

He said, 'Mamma, I never do nobody no evil. I never do nobody no wrong. Why would Jah give me cancer?'

After the initial shock, I tried to give him an answer. I replied, 'Nesta, I don't know. But Jah say who He loveth He chastiseth.'

We talked for about ten minutes. Nesta was fretting because he said the doctor in England wanted to cut off his foot. He said that he didn't know how he could perform without his foot, and I tried to reassure him and calm him down.

The call, when it ended, left me confused, upset, and heavy-hearted. How could Nesta, my son, known to the world as Bob Marley but to me from boyhood as 'Nesta', have cancer?

Nesta, whose name meant 'Messenger', had been born with song in his heart. His name and music were beloved throughout the world. He was a young man in the prime and glory of life. How could he be sick with cancer? And how could the cancer strike a part so small and puny as a big toe?

With this fresh burden on my heart, I returned to cooking

dinner – lima beans and rice – for Richard, Pearl and Anthony, my three other children.

Nesta had cancer?

Impossible.

The world knows me as Mother Booker (or Madda Booker, as Jamaicans say), and as I travel through my sixty-ninth year of life, many look to me as a mother. But every mother begins life as a daughter, and every daughter begins life as a child.

My own life began in 1926 with my birth in the mountainous bosom of Jamaica, in the district of Nine Miles, the parish of St Ann, where my family has lived from an unknown time for generations past. The nights are misty and cool, the days warm, and afternoon rains so plentiful that everywhere you look the slopes and hills are covered with thick, green woodlands. A single marl road winds through the district, linking Nine Miles with other hillside villages and with the sea-coast plains of Jamaica.

The people of our district dwell on the lush mountain slopes, keeping a few chickens, goats and pigs, and farming the terraces and hilltops with yam, corn and other ground produce for eating or selling in the market. Many of the houses are built on the hillside, but a few sip evening breezes off high mountain-tops.

The homes are modest, made of wood, mortar and stone, and built to straddle the slopes. All were lit by kerosene lamps and had cisterns or catchment basins built on to the mountainside to catch rainwater. During times of drought, we would go down into the valley, carrying kerosene cans on our heads, and draw water from a spring. The donkey was then the Volkswagen of transportation throughout the district, the horse the Cadillac.

Our house, though also without running water, had a shower on the lower floor that my father had rigged up from a water tank mounted in a room. Like the other dwellings, it had an outdoor pit toilet in the backyard.

My mother bore nine children, five boys and four girls: Enid, Ivy, Jonathan, David, Solomon, Cedella, Amy, Surgeon and Gibson. I was the sixth of nine, and the only girl to follow the birth of a boy, which may explain why during my childhood I always loved to fight. Mark you, I never went looking for a quarrel. But if trouble found me, whether in the shape of girl or boy, I always stood my ground.

I remember how one time, right in front of my father when my older brother was provoking me, I sprang up out of my chair and thumped him hard in the mouth. My father was so astonished that he bellowed and rushed outside to cut a switch.

'Imagine,' he roared, 'you jump up and thump you brother in him mouth right under me eye!'

He just couldn't believe that one of his daughters could be so wilful and rowdy.

My father was a man of many names. His given name was Omeriah. A strict, godly, kindly man of a medium build and dark complexion, he was looked up to by the people in the community, most of whom used to call him Custos, a term of respect used by Jamaicans. Some other people called him Mass Amy, short for Master Omeriah, and others called him Ma Name, which was one of his nicknames, but the majority called him Custos. Even though he was very stern with us, I loved my father deeply. To this day, everyone says that I resemble him more than all his other children.

Although he was not a church-going man, my father would sometimes read his Bible and tell us stories found in it and quote scriptures from its pages. He also had a dozen or more women in the district, who bore him between twenty and thirty children.

In fact, I know of three sisters in the district who had a total of nine children for my father. The oldest sister, whose name was Lizzy, had four; the second, Ruth, bore him two babies who lived and two who died; and the third, Blanche, had three children. All the children of my father, including those he had with his lawful wife, who was my mother, grew and played together in the same district of Nine Miles.

In addition to our house and its surrounding lands, my father owned another property of some thirty acres on a nearby mountain-top. On this property, which was named Smith, he had a house to which my mother never went because his other women might be up there, helping him farm. Every day when my father went up to work the lands of Smith, my mother, in turn, silently tended her own plot of ground around our house.

In our district my father, who was a clever man, owned one of the only Delco generators, which he would start up on Sundays whenever he wished to listen to the radio. Then friends and family would walk down from the hills and gather around on the verandah to listen to radio programs while all around us the still, green mountains stretched everywhere that eyeball could see. Sometimes we would hear a sermon from Kingston, sometimes rumba music from Cuba.

My father was very close to his mother, Yaya, and every morning before going to Smith, he would rise up out of his bed and walk up the hill to her house to drink coffee with her on her verandah. This habit continued throughout most of my life in Nine Miles, since Yaya lived long and walked the district until she bent.

My mother, whose name was Alberta but who was known as Miss B or Miss Berta, was a kindly, gentle woman with a charitable heart. Everyone in our district loved her. Many years after her death, people would come up to us and tell us of some little kindness she had done them.

The story in the family is that when my father got my mother pregnant, he was living with an older woman named Auntie My who used to labor in the hot sun beside him in the fields. My mother's father sent for him and told him that he had to do the right thing, and my father married my mother in a quiet wedding ceremony in Brown's Town and took her in his buggy to the house on the hillside that he shared with this older lady.

My mother walked bravely up the pathway to the house and said to an old lady she found sitting on the small wooden verandah, 'Good evening. I just want to let you know that I am now Mrs Malcolm.'

'Yes, Mum,' the old lady replied meekly, bowing her head. With that, she went inside, quietly gathered up all her personal belongings, and hurried away from the house she had helped my father build.

But she came back to visit my mother often, and soon became her helper in raising her children. I myself was this old lady's favorite and used to spend time with her at her own yard when I was a small child.

Sometimes my mother would become fed up with my father's women and return to the house of her own father. After she had been away a few days, my father would go up to that house and ask to have his wife back. One time when he went my mother's father spoke sharply to him, saying, 'Nobody ever run away from good. If you want her to stay with you, treat her good.'

One day I remember my mother was plaiting my hair on the verandah when one of my father's other women traipsed past and spat with scorn. My mother just continued to plait my hair and held her head high with pride and dignity and didn't give any rebuke. But later I heard her singing quietly to herself.

I don't know how my mother felt about my father's other women, except from what I glimpsed occasionally with my child's eyes over sixty years ago, but I do know that when the pressure got too much for her to bear, she would go alone to a place called Honeyland, which was her coffee field, and sing her heart out, and I would hear her beautiful voice echoing off the woodlands.

To this day, whenever I find myself feeling downhearted, I

follow the example of my mother and sing away my heart's troubles.

When I search my brain for my earlier childhood memories, I remember a strange weekend I spent at the house of a woman named Miss Katie Lawrence. Miss Katie was a woman who worked in my mother's shop and who took me as her favorite among all my mother's many children.

We had woken early that morning and Miss Katie had caught up a fire on the earth floor of the cooking shed to roast some cocoa for breakfast. She stepped outside to chat with one of her family when, drawn to the bright glow of the fire, I lit a splinter of wood and applied it to the thatch roof, telling myself that I was lighting my lamp. The dry strands of thatch flared up in a small fire that I quickly pinched out.

Then for some reason known to this day only to my four-year-old brain, I did it again, and this time the thatch ignited into a crackling blaze that quickly spread out of control. I ran outside and screamed, 'Miss Katie, de kitchen burn down, Ma'am! De kitchen burn down, Ma'am!'

Miss Katie and another woman raced inside and put out the blaze with water standing in a barrel outside the shed.

The great part about this memory, as I tell it now, is that I was not beaten for setting the thatch afire, but just scolded. Since we were always being beaten whenever we were bad, not to be beaten over something so serious was memorable enough to stick in my brain for over sixty years.

The custom in those days of my childhood was for any adult in the district who caught a child doing mischief to dish out a lick or two on the spot, to which the real mother, on hearing about the incident, might later add her own chastising blows.

Like any country child, I spent my early days romping between play-yard, church and school. I attended the Stepney school, where I learned early to read and write and developed a very good hand – so good, in fact, that I remember to this day that the first lesson I wrote in pen drew great praise from my teacher, who was a strict woman nicknamed 'Man Jackson' by the students behind her back.

When Man Jackson saw the text I had copied off the blackboard into my exercise book, she began to praise me lavishly about how well I had done for a first time – up to then we had written our lessons only on slate tablets, never with a pen. She took my book, crying, 'Miss Harvey! Come look at dis child's handwriting!' and showed it excitedly to the other teachers, who all came into the classroom to heap praise upon my head because of my lovely cursive hand.

But the very next time Man Jackson gave me an exercise to write, I just couldn't do it properly. I left out words and letters; my handwriting was no longer beautiful. I don't know whether the teachers had praised me too much and it had gone to my head, or whether I couldn't live up to their high expectations, but I spoilt the whole exercise. However, the teachers, when they found the fault in my next attempt at penmanship, didn't rough me up too bad, probably because they felt sorry for me.

Man Jackson, typical of her day, was a strict, no-joke teacher who used to walk around with a leather strap that she would use to beat her pupils. The strap was split at the end into four separate tails, and every blow from it carried the sting of four licks. She would beat us on our backs and shoulders and sometimes on our outstretched arms, splattering black and blue marks all over our bodies. When a big boy was dunce or misbehaved, she would march him into the vestry and make him strip off his pants. Then, with the boy folded over the back of a wooden bench, she would wale his naked buttocks with her four-tailed strap.

I remember one time when she beat me that I thought was very unfair. I had stayed home on a day that the education inspector for the district had come on a visit to our school and the class had skylarked and misbehaved, embarrassing Man Jackson. The next day, when I arrived at school, she marched us out into the yard and announced, 'All who were here yesterday, line up on my right. All who were absent, line up on my left.'

We milled about and formed two nervous lines in the school-yard, not knowing what to expect. Man Jackson then said, 'Those children who were here yesterday during the inspector's visit will get four strokes. Those who were absent will get two.' She proceeded to beat all of us with her four-tail strap. Those of us who had been absent that day, she gave two licks each 'in remembrance', she said, of the misbehavior.

I remember another incident when Man Jackson had beaten a number of the pupils: the next day some parents showed up at the school-yard to complain about welts she had left on their girl children. Many of the parents of that time didn't object if their boys were beaten in school, but would get upset if the same treatment was handed out to their daughters.

On this particular day, while the parents were raising their quarreling voices in the school-yard, Man Jackson rushed into her office, got her strap, came back out, charged the complaining mothers and began to beat them so hard that they ran off the hill, screaming. She was among the wickedest of a wicked crop of teachers who used to rule the lives of Jamaican children in country schools. The helpless mothers, having no one to appeal to, no telephone, no motorcar, no nearby Ministry of Education, just had to bear Man Jackson's licks and wander away down the unpaved country road, muttering angrily.

Eventually, Man Jackson was transferred from the Stepney school – most likely because of the many complaints – and her place taken by Teacher Palmer, who was also stern but more courteous and didn't murder the children with a four-tail strap over every little foolishness.

Today, because of the new laws, teachers at the Stepney school can no longer beat the children, many of whom don't even bother to attend school. The teachers seem as if they've said to themselves, 'Well, it's not my child, and it's not my brain, if dey want learn is all right, if dey don't want learn, is all right, too.'

Because of this new law and attitude, the children today seem less disciplined than we were, and uncaring about whether or not they learn to read and write.

One morning in 1935 we awoke to hear that the nearby district of Cave Valley had been flooded by heavy rain, and my father decided to drive his motorcar over there and have a look. At the time, he owned one of the only motorcars in the district. But before we went, my mother, who was heavy with her tenth child, called me into her room and groaned, 'Go up to Miss Maud and tell her to come to me. I don't feel well.'

I walked up the hill to Miss Maud's house and brought her back with me. Inside the room, my mother was complaining that her head hurt and that she felt sick, as if someone had 'marked a ten-cross over her forehead', which is a magical cross that can draw evil.

Miss Maud noticed that my mother had on a red handkerchief tied around her head and said, 'Miss Berta, take off de red tiehead. Maybe it draw de pain.' My mother did, but taking off the headtie didn't help.

My father and I left in his motorcar with some other men and drove to Cave Valley, where we saw that only the gullies were flooded and the water had not reached the road. On the way back a man named George Henry flagged us down at the bottom of the hill and said, 'Custos, your wife is on dying.'

My father raced up to the house and then quickly left in his motorcar to summon Dr Lloyd from the distant town of Claremont.

The next morning when I awoke, I heard a soft singing coming from the drawing-room. I tiptoed into the room to find several of my mother's sisters gathered in a solemn circle, singing the mournful song 'Blessed Hour of Prayer'. My heart beating fast, I rushed into my mother's bedroom and found her lying still, covered under the lumpiness of a bedsheet.

She had died during the night as I slept.

But I didn't believe she was dead, so I uncovered her toe and touched it. I cried, 'Her toe still warm! She no dead! Her toe warm!' But the adults poured into the bedroom and shooed me away from my mother's deathbed.

The doctor came later and took out a dead baby from my mother's body. He said the baby had been dead inside her for three days.

My father supervised the building of a cedar coffin and placed my dead mother inside it. By the tradition of the time, he did not work directly on the coffin himself, for that would look to the world as though he was taking an active hand in sending his wife away. I remember that we children took the shavings the carpenters had left behind from making the coffin and started a fire with them, saying that we were cooking our supper.

Some of the adults tried to stop us from burning the shavings off my mother's coffin, but my father, who was very down-hearted, just said heavily, 'Make dem stay!' and we were left with our game of cooking with firewood from my mother's coffin while the grown-ups went about the grim business of burial.

My mother was laid to rest that evening in a burial plot on our property. Not yet ten years old, I was left motherless on this earth.

Chapter Two

Mamma was dead. Puppa, as we used to call my father, was busy with his fields. Years later, he would marry a woman named Lurline Brown from Lucky Hill in the parish of St Mary, and she would move into my mother's room and sleep in my mother's bed.

I was now only ten years old and still attending school, but not happily. School was miles away down the country road, and even though I was a playful child who used to skip and run the whole way, it still took an hour or two to reach. In those days there was no bus, and the only transportation throughout the country parts of the island was what Jamaicans jokingly call footmobile – meaning you walked.

If we were late for school, the teachers wouldn't admit us to class and we would be left sitting on the banks of the roadside all day in the burning sun. Or, worse yet, we would be beaten for tardiness.

I just didn't like school. I didn't like being cooped up for hours under the rule of a sour-faced teacher like Man Jackson. I longed to escape the stuffy classroom and run around in the daylight breezes. Sometimes I would set out for school but never get there because I'd stop to romp in the fields all day with other children.

If my mother had been alive, she would have made me continue in school. But Mamma was gone and Puppa was a sympathetic man. If I cried that I didn't want to go to school one day, he would say, 'Don't force the child to go, if she don't want to.'

And that would be that.

One afternoon, shortly after the death of my mother, I was walking home from school when I saw my sister Amy on the hillside trail being picked on by a gang of upper-form bullies. Surrounded by her tormentors, she was crying and not fighting back.

Racing to her side, I picked up a stone and flung it point-blank into the face of the jeering ringleader, busting his head open with a splatter of blood. The other boys tried to gang up on me, but arming myself with rocks from the field, I stood my ground and dared them to come.

Eventually, after much bellowing of threats back and forth over the wails of the wounded ringleader, whose head was still gushing blood, my sister and I beat a retreat, leaving one boy bloody, his companions shrieking curses.

A few days later when I got word that the same boys were plotting to ambush me that morning on the road to school, I went to Puppa and said, 'Puppa, me a go follow you go a ground, sah,' meaning that I wanted to go with him that day into the fields, which was how I loved to spend my days.

He looked me over and said simply, 'Come on, nuh. Tie you head and come.'

I was then about ten years old. From that moment on my hated schooling was over for ever, and my daylight hours would be spent mainly in the fields beside Puppa.

Every day after that I followed Puppa to Smith, which was about three miles away up the mountain slope, and helped cultivate his land. Puppa always had men laboring in the fields of Smith, scattered around the hillside digging yam holes, clearing land for planting, or cutting bush for manure.

I spent my days carrying yam heads and dropping them on the yam banks for the laborers to plant. Sometimes I would spend the morning cutting and planting potato slips. On other days I would plant peas, or follow the men as they dug holes for me to plant corn. I would drop four grains of corn into each hole and cover it up with my bare foot, working my way up a hillside furrow.

I also began helping Puppa do the cooking, for the laborers had to be fed daily. We had a big three-foot pot in the kitchen at Smith, and every day we cooked up a meal the men would eat in the shade of a towering breadfruit tree where Puppa used to tie up his horses and donkeys.

When the pot of food was ready, Puppa would step outside the kitchen on to the hillside ground and bellow, 'Oh, sah! Oh, sah!' The laborers, at this call, would lay down their machetes and troop down the hillside to sit and eat lunch under the cool of the breadfruit tree.

It was in my daily trek to Smith that I began to take notice of a white man on a horse.

In our district a white man was a rare thing that drew the eye.

This one was an older man, then somewhere around fifty, and I used to see him daily riding his horse up and down the commons, hills and dirt roads.

People said he lived up in the settlement of Brisset, that he was an army officer in charge of parceling out the government lands of a place called John Williams to old soldiers. Everyone in the district addressed this white man as Captain. We found out that he was a white Jamaican, from the parish of Clarendon, and that his name was Norval St Clair Marley.

Our community was so small that everyone knew everyone either personally or through stories suss-sussed from mouth to earhole throughout the district. A funny story I heard about Captain came through Blanche, one of Puppa's women. She said that Captain had given a woman on the hillside a plantain to cook for him, that she had sliced it into four pieces, cooked them, and given him back three. Shortly afterwards, according to Blanche, Captain galloped his horse down to the woman's dwelling and demanded the fourth piece of his plantain.

We all laughed when we heard this story about Captain's stingy nature. Later on, I found out that Captain was really a kind and generous soul and that the story, which was whispered around to make fun of him, was probably false.

In the Jamaican countryside, even to this day, people often pass the long and idle evenings telling exaggerated stories about one another. And since Jamaicans believe that 'If it don't go so, it go near so,' meaning, if a story isn't exactly as it is told, it is nearly that way, once a story starts to make the rounds from verandah to verandah, even if it is untrue, it is likely to be believed. In Jamaica, no name or reputation escapes this idle tale-telling.

He came to our house every day, this Captain Marley, to sit on the verandah, smoke his pipe and have a chat with Puppa.

When I was still a little girl, he would often stop me in the hall or in the yard and ask me, 'Are you feathering yet?' Then he would give my breasts a playful pinch. Because of his antics, I used to run inside when I saw him riding down the road towards our house, but he would come into the kitchen to light his pipe and always either speak to me or run a joke.

I continued to grow, and soon I was sixteen and the whole world could see that I was now feathering. Suddenly a young woman filling out with her nature, I was not quite as keen about the sweaty labor in the fields of Smith, but was instead fussing with my appearance, brushing my hair, and checking my reflection often in a looking-glass.

Captain used to drop by more and more now, for he had recently moved into a nearby house on the hill that he rented from Yaya. He would stop and talk to me and ask why I didn't come to visit him at his house that night.

Sometimes I would say 'Yes,' I would visit him, but then I wouldn't go, and the next day when I saw him he would cut his eyes (glare out of the corner of his eye) at me in the way Jamaicans do when they're vexed. Or he would sulk and not talk to me, making me feel bad about the way I was treating him.

One late, late night I crawled out of my bed, climbed the hill in the pitch darkness, picking my footing by starlight, and paid Captain his midnight visit. I spent most of the night with him, slipping away early in the morning before anyone was awake and sneaking back into my own bed. Nobody in my house knew or saw or suspected.

That night with Captain was my first time ever with a man.

After that first time, Captain wasn't satisfied but wanted more and more.

He still dropped by to visit Puppa, but now he would be sure to take me aside and beg me in a whisper to come to him again. On one visit when he winked at me from the drawing-room, my sister Enid saw.

Awaking again in the pitch blackness a few nights later, I sneaked out of my room and climbed the hill in the darkness to Captain's house. My brother Surgeon, who shared the room with me, woke up, found me gone, and started to cry. Puppa, roused by my brother's sobbing, came from his side of the house to find out what had happened.

'Ciddy not here,' my brother blubbered. 'Ciddy gone!'

'What!' Puppa exclaimed.

He woke up my brother Gibson, and they lit lamps and began combing the house for me. They went from room to room and, not finding me, were stumped about where to search next when Enid, who remembered Captain's wink, said, 'You know, maybe she could be over Captain's.'

At that, Puppa and my brother Gibson stormed out into the night and up the darkened hill to pound on Captain's front door.

They caught us both fast asleep.

Inside, facing the wall and in a dead sleep beside Captain, I sprang up at the deafening pounding and in my confusion kept bucking my head against the wall as I tried to scramble out of bed while Puppa banged so loudly on the door that Captain's little wooden house shivered like it suffered night fever.

'Ciddy in dere?' Puppa bellowed.

'Yes! Yes!' the flustered Captain answered, trying to climb out of bed in shock.

'Open up!' Puppa roared.

By then I was out of bed, and before Puppa could catch me, I had flung open the front door, flashed past him in the darkness and was blowing like a breeze down the hill. I could hear male voices raised in anger behind me in the night. Scrambling down the trail, I rushed into my room, grabbed a small grip I kept under my bed, tossed a few possessions into it, and flew out into the darkness to crawl and hide in the cellar.

I could hear Puppa raging to Miss Lurline in his bedroom. 'Dat little wretch! You know where she was? Over Captain's.'

'What you saying?' Miss Lurline exclaimed.

'You wait till daylight!' Puppa vowed angrily.

I cowered in the cellar until the angry muttering had died down and everybody was once again asleep. It was so dark where I was hiding that I couldn't even see my hand held right in front of my eyes.

I carefully felt my way out of the cellar, put the grip atop my head, and headed off down the country road in the darkness.

Fearful and anxious, I walked for hours, meeting not a single soul along the dark road. The surrounding fields and mountains were blurry in the night-time mist, and every step I took made a noisy crunch on the marl. I kept eyeing the dark woodlands for signs of life, tormenting my brain about what I would do if I met up with a rolling calf, which was the devil in the body of a fiery-eyed cow.

Hours later, the long night gave way to day and I found myself at Alva and the house of my maternal grandfather, whose name was Uncle Dan. It was dawn. The birds were just waking up and beginning to make their first daylight noises.

'Daughter, what bring you here so early?' Uncle Dan asked with astonishment when I showed up in the first light at his doorstep.

I began to cry, showing him my little sorry self. 'A me modder-in-law tell lie 'pon me,' I sobbed, 'an' mek me daddy beat me.'

'Tell lie 'pon you?' Uncle Dan cried. 'Poor you! Poor you! What you do?'

'Me no do nothing!' I bawled. 'Me no do nothing!'

'Well,' Uncle Dan said wearily, 'if you come, me nah throw you out. I don't know de fullness of what happen, but you me grandpickney, and me nah throw you out.'

And so I was able to stay with him for a few days, helping around the house and hiding from Puppa's wrath.

On the third day, Captain rode up on his horse. I don't know how he had found out where I was, but I was not surprised to see him, for our community was very small.

'You've got to go home, Ciddy,' he begged me. 'Your father says he's going to take me to court and sue me because you're under age. You've got to go home, Ciddy. They're going to kill me if you don't.'

Captain was a man who loved to cry, as I had by then found out, and whenever his heart was troubled over any little foolishness, eyewater would flow. That day while he was begging me to return home and telling me how he was living in direct hell, plenty water dropped from his blue eyes. But I was still terrified of Puppa and ashamed because everyone in the district knew what I had done. I refused to go home, no matter how hard Captain begged.

The next day Captain came again and implored me to return home, saying that he wasn't leaving without me. He explained the trouble to Uncle Dan, who was also of the mind that I should return to Puppa's house.

To avoid facing Puppa, I was prepared to try anything. In my desperation, I even followed up a tip my Aunt Lou gave me about a minister, one Brother Wright, who lived alone in Clarendon and needed someone to take care of him.

A few days later, I set out on the dirt road to visit Brother Wright. I walked the whole way with my cousin Boise, who was going to take a donkey down from the man's property back to St Ann.

Brother Wright turned out to be an old white man in a straw hat who said he couldn't pay me for taking care of him other than with room and board but that I could pick all the fruit I wanted from his property and sell it on the roadside. Being alone on a faraway hill with this strange man and no other woman nearby didn't appeal to me, but I said I would consider the offer, and trudged back down the road beside Boise, drifting gloomily towards Puppa's house, not knowing what to do or where to go.

We were taking turns walking and riding the donkey back to Alva, when we came across a part of the road that coils around a series of hills, and I glimpsed Puppa and brother Gibson approaching on bicycles around a distant corner. Jumping over the bank of the roadway, I crawled under the overhanging bushes and hid under the lip of dirt.

Puppa rode up and I heard him demand, 'Where is Ciddy?'

'Me don't know, sah,' Boise lied.

'She must be somewhere 'bout de place you know, sah,' Gibson added. He began throwing rockstones into the bushy embankment to flush me out, but because I was hugging the overhang, they sailed over my head and fell harmlessly into the bush.

After they had left and Boise assured me that the coast was clear, I crawled out from hiding, and plodded fearfully across the commons towards my grandfather's house.

A few days later Captain came galloping across the fields to my grandfather's house, dismounted and began weeping, begging me to return home, saying he would do anything if I obeyed him. But I was stubborn and afraid of Puppa.

Captain, however, was determined. He said this was now courthouse business, that if I didn't return home with him this very night, my father would prosecute him. He begged and begged. I was of one mind and then another. Uncle Dan advised me to go. Finally, I got worn down by all Captain's begging. As night was falling, I agreed to go back with him, and we set out in the twilight for Nine Miles.

We trudged across the commons, Captain and I, making our way slowly and heavily towards Puppa's house. As the guinea grass of the commons parted before us, I wondered what Puppa would do. Would he beat me with a switch? What would he say? What would my family say? What would I do, if I didn't go home? I couldn't go and live in Clarendon with Brother Wright because there was something about him I didn't trust. But where would I sleep? And how would I eat?

Several times along the way, Captain got off his horse and invited me to mount up and ride, but I said 'No.' So we crossed the commons and before I knew it, we had reached the outskirts of our property and my house lay just over the hill. I could see the lights of the settlement glittering against the dark bulk of the mountain. Making up my mind, and without another word to Captain, I took a deep breath and raced across the mountain slopes and ran inside my house, where I sneaked into my sister's room and hid.

Captain rode up to the verandah, got off his horse, and went inside where I heard him say to Puppa, 'I bring you daughter home, sah.' Then he got on his horse and rode away.

Later that night Puppa appeared in the doorway of my sister's room and looked long and hard at me as I quailed in a far corner. He said he heard I'd gone to Clarendon.

I said meekly, 'Yes, sah.'

He said he didn't trust that minister man and was glad I'd come home and not gone to work for him.

I replied, 'Yes, Puppa.'

Another hard look and Puppa walked heavily away.

That night, with a giddy sense of relief and joy, I slept soundly again in my own childhood bed.

Early the next morning Puppa sent for Captain and me, calling the two of us into his room while my sisters peeped timidly in at the conference from every window.

At first Puppa was very stern, telling Captain that he had to be responsible for anything that happened to me because I was under age. Captain agreed he would be responsible.

'Ciddy,' Puppa asked me, 'you love Captain?'

'Yes, sah,' I whispered.

'Captain,' he asked gruffly, 'you love Ciddy?'

Captain said he did.

Puppa asked if he intended to marry me but Captain said 'No,' he couldn't do that just now. Puppa said that he agreed for he thought I was too young to marry.

'All right, then,' Puppa declared. 'Ciddy is belonging to you. You are fully responsible for her from now on, since she loves you, and you love her. Understand?'

Captain nodded.

'She's living under my roof,' Puppa continued, 'so I will feed her. She can stay here. But everything else is your responsibility. Understand?'

Captain said he did.

From that moment on – as witnessed and no doubt suss-sussed about in our district that very day by my peeping sisters – our whole world knew that, although only sixteen, I was now the woman of Captain Norval St Clair Marley.

Chapter Three

For a while things between me and Captain ran smoothly. He continued to visit Puppa at evening time, to sit on the verandah, cock up his foot on the railing, smoke his pipe and chat about happenings in the district. At night I would sometimes climb the hill to sleep in Captain's arms.

I began to learn about Captain and his ways.

I found out that he was a moody man, or, as country people say, a man with 'Quicksilver inna him head', meaning one with a changeable nature. Sometimes when villagers would stroll past Captain sitting on the verandah and say, 'Good evening, Captain,' for no reason at all he would just cut his eye at them and look cross. Other times he would warmly greet the passer-by and invite him to sit and chat.

I also learned that years ago Captain had gotten a maid pregnant who used to work for his mother. After she got pregnant, according to Captain, the maid became frightened and left the job to return to her home in the country. He said he eventually found out that she had borne him a daughter and named her Constance.

Years afterwards when Bob was living with me in Delaware, this same Constance sent him a letter. Bob read it and said to me, 'She say she me sister. And she name Constance.'

I replied, 'Yes, your father told me about her. Write her back.'

'Me can't write her back,' Bob said. 'Me no know what to write her say.'

'Just write her,' I urged him. 'Don't just put de letter down. Write her back.'

And he did. Years later he even got to meet his sister Constance face to face when she paid him a visit in Jersey.

So Captain and I went along for a while, and the road between us was more or less smooth.

Then I caught religion. And the road turned rocky.

One evening I attended service at the Shiloh Apostolic church and witnessed a powerful exaltation that shook me down to my very bones. It was given by a girl even younger than me named Vinette Callum. Hearing her read the scripture and speak the exaltation made my knees tremble with a terrible weakness as I was struck by a powerful longing to repent. When she gave the altar call, moaning, 'Jesus is calling the weary to rest! Calling today! Calling today!' I clenched my teeth and fought against the call, gripping the bench, singing, and openly weeping.

But there was no opposing the call the next night: I surrendered and went weeping to the altar to be saved. I had gone over to the church. And Elder Thomas made it plain to me that a woman who was saved could not lie with a man unless he was her lawful husband. If she did, she committed the sin of fornication, which the Bible describes as a great wickedness.

At first I could not bring myself to tell Captain the news about my conversion. When he would ask me to come and visit him, I would make an excuse or cook up some explanation the next day of why I hadn't showed. Eventually, however, the truth came out: I told Captain that because I was now saved, I could no longer come to him at night.

He got vexed and started one piece of cussing. He said that parsons carried dust in their pockets that they sprinkled over church sisters, making them fall down and bawl out that they were saved. That way the parsons got the women for themselves.

'I don't want you going to dat goddamn fucking church,' he

railed. 'Everybody know dat parson man carry change inna dem pocket to go tecky-tecky and bamboozle fool-fool church woman.'

But my mind was made up. I was with the church. My nights of fornicating with Captain were over.

War broke out between us.

Captain ran to complain to Puppa, who laughed and said jokingly to him, 'Well, Captain, you just have to give her a whipping if she won't obey you.'

Afterwards, Puppa rebuked me over the way I was treating Captain, telling me that for a woman to withhold intercourse from her man was a sin. I answered him with the argument that for such withholding to be a sin the woman had to be lawfully married, but for an unmarried woman to otherwise have sexual relations was fornication. Puppa went away, muttering.

Captain tried his best to talk me out of my new beliefs, and he would often ride up to the house in a quarrelsome mood.

'You still going to dat goddamn fucking church?' he would ask.

'Yes, I am,' I would reply calmly. 'I am saved.'

'Saved!' he would bawl. 'Saved my foot!'

Then he would cuss bad words, saying many wicked things about the church and its parson. He began to pay the village boys four pence each to go to the service and, in his words, 'Mash up dat goddamn fucking church!'

Sometimes the boys would troop in and sit in the back pews and make up some little noises during the service, but Elder Thomas would rage at them immediately, 'Out! Out, you little imps!'

The boys would proudly report to Captain that they had mashed up the service on Sunday, and Captain would dig into his pocket for their 'mash-up-church' money and pay them off, saying, 'Good boys! Good boys! Do it again next Sunday! Mash it up! Mash it up good!'

'Yes, sah!' the boys would grin. 'We goin' go dere and raise hell!'

And they would try, too, until they were stopped by Elder's chastising roar, 'Out! Out, you little imps!' which would send them scampering out of the church and into the fields.

Captain's mash-up-the-church plan, however, didn't work. I attended services faithfully. I sang in the choir. I became a popular soloist and sang hymns accompanied by a guitarist. One time, for example, Elder Thomas took me on a village concert and I sang, 'I can see everybody's mother, but I don't see mine,' and when I was done, there wasn't a dry eye in the audience. My singing had such a powerful effect that I gave encores. The men in the audience vowed that my foot would not touch the ground when I left the hall, that they would carry me off the hill, but Elder Thomas said such treatment was unnecessary, that I could walk like everyone else. The villagers made Elder Thomas promise to bring me back to sing for them again. Even today, I keenly remember how the praise sweeted me and made me glad.

I loved everything about the church. I loved to hear the exaltations. I loved the dancing, the singing, the witnessing, the public repenting, the speaking in tongues. I loved the drumming, the sight of the worshipping women in their pretty white dresses, the grave and proper air of the elders. I always came away from services with lightness and joy in my heart. I was even hoping that one day I would soften Captain up and lead him weeping to the altar to repent.

Puppa, meanwhile, had taken Captain's side with a vengeance and was stern against the church. One evening as I got ready to go to service, Puppa said to me, 'No, you not goin'!'

'Yes, sah, I am going,' I protested.

'I said no!' he thundered.

I began to cry as I saw the sisters dressed in white filing past our house towards the church. I cried for a long, long time that cheerless evening.

'Because of money, I must lose my soul!' I wailed to my father, making him feel very bad as I could see in his face when he stood in the doorway of my bedroom that evening, looking ashamed and sorry.

But I had spoken the wrong word. It wasn't money that made Puppa take Captain's side, for Captain was a poor man. It was their old-time friendship. Plus I think that my conversion must have struck a nerve deep inside Puppa, who could well imagine how miserable his own life would become if his many women suddenly gave up fornication.

Captain, meanwhile, got more vexed and more demanding. One day I was in the fields of Smith with my sister Amy, spreading out coffee beans to dry in the sun, when I heard hoof-beats and looked up to see Captain approaching on horseback.

He hitched up his horse and came strolling over to us. Suddenly, he was standing over me and before I could even greet him, he began to lash me with the supplejack he used to control his horse, raging, 'I told you to stop going to dat goddamn fucking church.'

He gave me four hot licks with the supplejack. I began to cry and so did sister Amy. When his rage had quieted, he snarled, 'Your father say to give you a good horsing! Now stop going to dat goddamn fucking church!' Then he mounted his horse and rode away over the brow of the hill, leaving me and my sister weeping.

The next day I was in my backyard when Captain rode up again. He came around to where I was and asked me for a stick of fire to light his pipe. I took one out of the stove and handed it to him. Staring at me with a mischievous grin, he jabbed the firestick towards me as if he would burn me.

'Put it inna de fire youself,' I said.

He gave me a rough shove. 'Who you think you talking to?' he growled.

I reared back and slammed my fists hard against his chest, pitching him over backwards and sending him sprawling flat on the ground.

Miss Lurline Brown heard the noise and came running over. 'No, no, no, no, Ciddy!' she begged. 'Don't trouble him!'

'If you think you bad,' I warned Captain, pointing at him as he scrambled to his feet, 'you touch me again!'

He looked shocked, muttered a curse, mounted his horse and rode away.

That was the last time Captain ever tried to lay a finger on me.

He kept away after that for a long while.

Sometimes he would pass the house and not stop, and I would glimpse him riding down the road and disappearing into a glen or over a hill. People began to remark at his absence. Miss Lurline even said to me one day after watching Captain ride past without stopping, 'It seems as if Captain found a new found out,' meaning that he had gotten another woman.

'Maybe so,' I replied, watching him. 'I don't know.'

But this phase did not last, and soon he began to stop again, begging a firestick to light his pipe or sitting down to chat with Puppa. And when Captain next spoke to me, he used a new approach: he told me he was sick with a thing called hernia, and that sometimes it swelled up on him. He said the doctors wanted to cut him but were worried because of his age.

He had moved in with Yaya by then and was living at her house, and when he told me that he was unwell and began to cry, I took pity on him. With tears in his eyes, he begged me to come and visit him that night when I was done working at

Smith. I said I would stop by and see him, and that night I did.

I sat at his bedside while Yaya served him bush tea to help his hernia. Then she closed the door and left us alone. Captain began to hug me and talk about his upcoming operation and sweet-mouth me about how much better he felt now that I was here holding his hand at his bedside. The honey poured plentiful and thick out of his mouth.

I gave in. That night Bob was conceived. And Captain knew Bob was coming, for the next morning when he awoke he told me I was pregnant.

'Pregnant?' I blurted, still groggy with sleep. 'How you know?'

He said that when the seed left his body, a man could tell right away if it had found fertile soil. He was sure that I was pregnant.

But I didn't believe him, and I sneaked out of his room that morning, feeling deeply ashamed. After resisting temptation now for so many months, I was silently lashing myself for backsliding into fornication. But a crying man will melt the hardest woman's heart.

The very next month I missed my period. I was pregnant with Bob.

Shortly after I got pregnant, Captain decided that because of his hernia he could no longer ride his horse and needed some other kind of work. He found a job as construction foreman for a bridge-building firm in Kingston and announced that he was leaving the district.

One evening as I came down from working all day at Smith, Captain rode up and said he wanted to talk to me. He walked by my side and told me that he was going to get married.

'Married?' I cried. 'Married to who?'

'To you,' he said calmly.

'I can't marry,' I replied, 'I'm too young.'

'No, you're not,' Captain said. 'I'll talk to your father. You're carrying my child. I'm leaving for Kingston this weekend and before I go, I want to marry you.'

True to his word, Captain spoke to my father and made the arrangements, and that Friday, 9 June 1944, a small group of family and friends gathered on Yaya's verandah to witness the marriage between me and Captain. Parson Aljoe of the Stepney Baptist church spoke the words. I wore a white dress, white hat and white stockings, but brown shoes. Captain wore a tweed suit. The wedding party celebrated by eating bread, for we had no wedding cake.

But the wedding did not pass without a fuss.

A woman from our district named Lucy Lawrence who claimed to have borne a son for Captain – which he staunchly denied – strolled up to the verandah after the wedding, cut me up and down with her grim stare and snapped, 'So you married today! But remember dis: what sweet nanny goat goin' run him belly!'

Captain had gone to walk Parson Aljoe to his buggy pulled up on the roadside and wasn't there to witness this scene, but I told him about it afterwards.

'Don't pay her no mind,' he warned. 'Dat is a evil woman.'

He swore that he didn't even know if Lucy Lawrence was a woman or a man, that she bore him an unknown grudge, had tried to blame him for making her pregnant, and was always trying to pick fights with him. Captain said that her baby-father was the young son of a Chinyman she had once worked for, but the boy wouldn't accept the responsibility.

On Saturday, the day after our wedding, Captain departed for Kingston. That Sunday, Lucy Lawrence paraded boastfully past our house. Beside her trotted her donkey, loaded up to the skies with her life's treasures.

Everybody in our district immediately started suss-sussing. 'Captain left yesterday, and Lucy left today,' they remarked, 'de two o' dem going live together in Kingston.'

I didn't know what to think. But I put out of mind the obvious evil everyone else was imagining.

Lucy Lawrence ended up in Kingston selling mangoes off Windward Road, where my cousin Doris spotted her one day, her wares spread out on the sidewalk. A couple of months later, Lucy Lawrence was murdered, her body thrown over a bridge and down a gully. Still puffed-up with money, her higgler's thread-bag dangled untouched from her neck; her unsold mangoes were still stacked in neat piles on the pavement. She had been stabbed savagely. No one was ever arrested for her murder.

Now a grown man, her son to this day tells the world that he is Bob Marley's brother.

Chapter Four

During the time that I carried Nesta, Captain and I corresponded regularly, but he came to see me only twice during those long months.

I continued to go up to Smith with my father until I grew so big that I could no longer work in the fields. I began to dream regularly about the child I was carrying, and in my dream, which I had often, I was always giving birth to two babies with wavy hair and a straight nose. I visioned the baby clean and beautiful, with no germs on his head and with a beautiful nose – always a beautiful nose.

Before he left, Captain scraped together every penny he had and gave it to my father to build a little house for me up on the hill near where Yaya lived. I soon moved into it to await the arrival of my baby. It was in this same house that Nesta was raised and beside which he now sleeps the endless sleep in his tomb.

As I grew bigger and bigger, the women of my district began to warn me that without a husband in my bed to keep me open, I would have a hard delivery. I wrote and expressed my worry to Captain about what they were saying, but he wrote me back and said that they were fool-fool country women who didn't know what they were talking about, that I'd be fine.

I took him at his word. We wrote letters back and forth. I made clothes for my baby. I did small chores around the house. I waited. And I worried, for in my thinking I was still a child and had no true idea of childbirth.

But Puppa knew. One day he handed me a big doctor book, saying, 'You have to pray a lot, and read, for even though you are here, in your condition you stand between life and death. Read dis doctor book.'

Many times during my pregnancy, if he caught me idling or romping, he would give me the same stern warning about being between 'life and death' and urge, 'Read de doctor book. Read de doctor book.'

Because Puppa frightened me so, I did try a few times to read that big, old-time doctor book, but I couldn't make head or tail of it. So I put it aside and dreamed dreams about my baby and wrote letters to Captain and waited.

During these days, I used to have bad dreams about Lucy Lawrence. In these terrible dreams, she was always threatening me and my unborn child. I had one especially bad dream about her brother, Caleb Lawrence, who chopped up two people with his machete and was hanged. In this fearful dream, he was armed with a penknife and searching for me, and I just barely missed meeting up with him on the street.

Then one night I had a vision that put my fears at rest. I was alone in my room, sleeping to the dim glow of a blue lamp Captain had given me, when a woman dressed in white appeared in the darkness and whispered, 'Dem can't trouble you, you know.' I stared at her. She seemed to glow and then softly fade away like a dying fire. Just then, the blue lamp grew bright on its own, and the room was brushed with the flickering kerosene light. After that, I wasn't afraid any more.

My baby was under the protection of powers and would be safe. When my time came, the midwife would take care of everything. She would come into the room with me, and she would do all the work for the baby to be born. And that would be that.

Or so I foolishly thought.

My sister Amy, perhaps, knew better. At least she prepared better than I did. She poured kerosene oil into a bottle and pushed a wick made out of paper down its neck. Then she put the makeshift lamp on the dresser, saying that if I had my baby at night, this would be our light.

A few nights later, by the flickering glow of Amy's homemade lamp, Nesta was born.

I went into labor on Sunday, 4 February 1945, when the first cramps struck during daytime church service. I was on and off in labor the entire day and into the night. Monday, when we had fasting in our church, I stood in the pews, trying not to double over to the pangs of labor.

I returned home and sent for Auntie Missy, my grandfather's sister, who was a midwife, and she attended me. But she wasn't doing the work as I thought she would, and I lay moaning on the bed with labor pains and wondering what had gone wrong.

Auntie Missy pointed to some old pictures of women on the wall of the room and said sternly, but kindly, 'See all those pictures on de wall of all doze pretty lady? Everyone of dem had to go through what you're going through here.'

'But it not supposed to go so,' I wailed. 'Why you not doing de proper work? Why you not having de baby?'

'Push,' she commanded, rubbing my belly with oil. 'Push.'

'Me to push?' I bawled. 'Why you not doing de pushing?'

That night I learned the meaning of *labor*. And after hours of pain and suffering, I did manage one final, mighty push, and a beautiful baby boy with a straight nose came into the world the way all life begins, from the womb of a suffering woman.

He was the loveliest boy child I had ever seen, and his entire family dwelling on the mountain slopes of Nine Miles was awake and waiting to greet him in the darkness of that damp, misty morning. My sisters were all awake and lining up at my bedside along with Puppa and his new wife, Lurline Brown, to give my newborn son hugs.

Everyone agreed that this child was beyond beautiful and wanted to hold and kiss him. That night as I lay exhausted in my bed, weary down to my every bone, I cradled my newborn son in my arms, put him to the' breast, and felt the power and glory known only to women who bring new life into this old world.

My father telegraphed Captain with the news, and a few days later he came to shower his newborn son with love and kisses. He held him in his arms and walked the floor proudly and told me that he would name him Nesta Robert Marley – the middle name being his younger brother's.

'Nesta?' I griped. 'I don't like dat name. People goin' call him "Lester". I know plenty man name "Lester".'

'Not "Lester",' Captain corrected me, still striding back and forth with his son in his arms, 'N-e-s-t-a.'

'Nesta?' I squawked. 'Where dat name come from?'

'It's a name I like,' Captain said. 'That will be his name.'

It was a funny name, and at first I didn't like it, but I felt that Captain had the right to name his own son, so I agreed. Later I found out that the name meant 'Messenger', but whether or not Captain knew that when he christened his son 'Nesta', I don't know.

Of course, Puppa's heart brimmed with joy over the birth of his first grandson, but Captain's family did not share his feeling. Captain was not a man to talk much about his private troubles, but it came out during the visit that he had been recently disinherited by his mother.

His mother had two sons, Robert, who was a well-known engineer, and Captain. Robert had two sons of his own. Captain's mother had changed her will, leaving all her worldly goods to Robert's two sons. Captain told me that under the new will, he would not get a penny.

At first Captain didn't want to say that his mother had disinherited him because he'd married a black woman. But this revelation soon came out. Later he changed the story and claimed that she was vexed not because his wife black, but because he had gotten married without telling her.

To this day, I don't know the true story. All I know is that Nesta came and left this world loved everlastingly by my family but shunned by his father's. And the hardship of being disinherited would fall most heavily not on Nesta, but on Captain, whose family treated him harshly after our marriage.

Captain stayed with me and Nesta a week, and then he returned to his work in Kingston, leaving me in the hillside house with our new son.

Nesta grew normally like any other baby, fussy sometimes, cooing and gurgling on the bed sometimes, sleeping on and off through night and day. When he cried for feeding, I would put him to my breast and sing to him and tell him stories. I wrote regularly to Captain, giving reports and news about his son, and he would always answer me back, asking questions that showed his concern.

And then when Nesta was about six months old something puzzling happened.

One day after feeding him, I placed him on the floor, propped up between pillows, while I went to work on a sewing machine patching a pair of pants for my brother Gibson. After I had worked on the pants for a while, I got hungry and, leaving Nesta briefly on the floor, stepped out into the yard and walked to my father's roadside shop to ask Lurline Brown to sell me a bun and a soft drink for lunch.

I was gone only a couple of minutes, but when I returned to the house, I found Nesta had fallen over and was sprawled out on the floor between the pillows. I picked him up and tried to burp him, thinking that maybe he had gas, and after patting his back, I returned him to the pillows.

He immediately vomited a watery fluid. I picked him up and found that he barely had life in him, that his eyes were rolling back in their sockets.

Mad with fright, I hollered for my stepmother and my sister Enid. 'Come quick!' I screamed. 'De baby sick! De baby sick!'

They rushed into the room and Miss Lurline, after one glance at the baby, nodded and muttered ominously, 'De baby well sick. Him sick, sick.'

My stepmother rushed to send a telegram to Captain. I called out to a man named Squire Rob who was working in our yard, crying, 'Beg you run up to Smith and call Puppa. Tell him Nesta sick! Hurry! Quick, quick!'

Squire jumped on his bicycle and raced up the mountain trail to Smith, and after a little while, Puppa came tearing down the slopes on the same bicycle and rushed into my room to find Nesta in my arms, limp and gasping weakly for life.

After one quick look at Nesta, who lingered on death's door-step, Puppa said, 'Evil spirits play wid de baby.'

He rushed out into his fields and returned with herbs that he had boiled up in a pot and told me to get the baby to drink the warm liquid. 'After him drink,' Puppa said, 'him goin' throw up, and whatever evil spirits inside him, goin' come out. Den he will feel better.' Puppa then used a piece of clothes blue and marked a ten-cross under Nesta's arms and on his foot-bottoms to keep the evil spirits from further troubling him.

I gave Nesta Puppa's drink, trying my best to force it down his throat, while his head flopped lifelessly from side to side in my arms, and eventually I succeeded and he swallowed feebly.

'When de baby throw up de evil,' Puppa ordered, 'give him some mint tea to drink.' Then Puppa left to return to Smith.

A few minutes after being force-fed Puppa's medicine, Nesta began vomiting violently. Out of his mouth and bottom spewed a slime thick like starch. It was a nasty, raw, rotten matter, and it gushed out of his body like it spewed from every pore. Later,

I would have to wash his diapers three or four times before I got down to the fabric, the slimy coating was so curdled and thick.

Yaya, who had heard the news, came bawling down the hill, 'Oooh! Oooh! Dey kill de man one pickney! Dey kill de man one pickney!' She burst into the room, weeping and wailing, expecting to find her great-grandson dead, but found him, instead, vomiting up slime and fighting for life. She immediately set to work, making up a little thread-bag with a string that closed it. Inside the bag, which she carefully tied around Nesta's neck, she placed some herbs and weeds that would drive away evil.

Nesta recovered. After throwing up the slime and drinking the mint tea, he fell into a deep and peaceful sleep. We sent a telegram to Captain, telling him that his son had gotten better, and a few days later he journeyed from Kingston to see for himself. He found a happy, healthy country baby, cooing on the floor between the pillows. Around his neck dangled Yaya's bag of potions.

Puppa, renowned through the district as a bush doctor and herbalist, had saved my first-born, Nesta Robert Marley, the only child I would ever bear for Captain.

Chapter Five

Captain did not prove himself a good father. Mostly, he stayed away from his son, writing the occasional letter but visiting only rarely. He seemed to take little or no interest in Nesta's upbringing.

When Nesta turned four, I registered him in the Stepney school to begin his schooling under Teacher Isaacs, who had replaced Teacher Palmer. During those days I used to keep a little roadside shop near the school, and I could sometimes look out the window and see the children learning their lessons outdoors. Many times I would glimpse Nesta teaching the other children how to form their letters or how to count, for he was already marked by his teachers from those early days as exceedingly bright and was allowed to tutor the slower pupils.

Captain, meantime, continued his neglectful ways. On one of his rare visits he told me bluntly, 'My brother wants to adopt Nesta. The only thing is, you're not going to ever see him again. It'll be like he's yours no more.'

His brother Robert was the one after whom Nesta had gotten his middle name. Captain had earlier brought up the subject with Puppa, who had warned me what was coming.

'No,' I said. 'I don't want nobody adopt my child.'

'They'll take good care of him,' Captain insisted. 'They'll give him opportunities.'

'We take good enough care of him down here,' I answered. 'Life will provide him with opportunities.'

The whole story struck me as funny. Here Captain's mother

had disinherited him because he had married a black woman. She did not even know Nesta, her own grandson, and had never tried to see him. Now, all of a sudden, Captain's brother, her other son, a wealthy and famous engineer in Jamaica, wanted to adopt Nesta and take him away from me and mine.

Over my dead body.

With that answer, Captain never again brought up the subject.

Nesta continued to grow and develop as a happy country child, loved by his family and friends and admired by his teachers.

He was going on six years old and progressing very well in his daily lessons under Teacher Isaacs when Captain came to me and said that he was arranging, at his expense, for Nesta to attend boarding school in Kingston.

Nesta's teachers were dead set against the idea from the start. 'Mrs Marley,' Teacher Isaacs warned me one day in the village street, 'I think it is a very bad thing for Nesta to leave the school here and go to Kingston. The teaching that children get in the country is better than in Kingston and more progressive. I wish you would reconsider.'

I said that I appreciated her concern, but I had to respect the wishes of his father. She was glum during the conversation and muttered that the Kingston influence would spoil all the good Nesta had gotten from his country schooling.

So over the objections of his teachers, I packed Nesta's bags; his father came to get him, and one afternoon, the two of them departed for Kingston.

Months went past, months and months. During that time I heard nothing from Nesta or about Nesta. I wrote Captain letter after letter for news about our son and got no answer. Day and night passed with no word, and I was beginning to fret.

Finally, I posted a strong letter to Captain, declaring my intention to travel to Kingston and see Nesta no matter what. Captain quickly wrote me back to say that Nesta was in boarding school in the parish of St Thomas, not in Kingston, and that he was being taught by a good teacher and progressing well in his lessons.

I was glad to hear the news but still worried and puzzled about why I had heard nothing from either Nesta or his teacher. Where exactly was Nesta? He wrote a child's scrawl, but he could still write to his mother. Why hadn't he written? What had happened to my son?

Months passed with no answer.

However, Jah moves through life in mysterious ways.

One evening Maggie Simpson, a higgler from our district who used to travel all over the island buying and selling goods, dropped into my shop with the news that she had just seen Nesta on a Kingston street.

'What?' I exclaimed, nearly falling off my shopkeeper's stool with shock.

'Yes, I saw Nesta, Auntie Ciddy,' she said, using my nickname.

'Where?'

She explained that as she was traveling somewhere off Spanish Town Road she heard someone calling, 'Miss Maggie! Miss Maggie!' and when she turned around, Nesta was standing in the street, grinning at her.

'What you say?' I cried. 'How him look?'

'Him look good,' she assured me. 'Me telling you de truth. Him look good. Him fat and him have on clean clothes.' She added that Nesta said that he was on his way to the market to buy charcoal for one Miss Gray, and that he had sent a message for me.

'What message?' I asked eagerly.

'Him say, "Tell me modder to come look for me,"' she replied.

'Look for him? Look for him where?'

'Him say him live on Haywood Street.'

'Which part of Haywood Street?'

'Auntie Ciddy, me telling you de God truth: me no remember. But him say him definitely live on Haywood Street.'

My brain was in a whirl. How could Nesta be living on Haywood Street in Kingston when he was supposed to be at boarding school in St Thomas? Who was this Miss Gray who had sent my son to buy charcoal?

Maggie Simpson told me that her cousin Merle had been with her when Nesta had come running up to them, and perhaps she would remember where on Haywood Street he said he lived. As soon as Maggie left my shop, I wrote a letter to Merle and walked it over to the Post Office so it would go out that afternoon on the mail bus.

A few days later Merle wrote back and said she couldn't recollect the address Nesta had given them, but that Haywood Street was a short street and if I traveled to Kingston she would meet me, and we could walk it together and inquire after him.

I quickly wrote her back telling her when I would be arriving, and a few days later I got on to the bus for Kingston and set out in search of Nesta.

I reached Kingston late in the afternoon just as the shops were shuttering up for the night, met Merle, and we started walking up and down Haywood Street, asking bystanders and market people if they had seen a little boy named Nesta Marley running around the neighborhood. Eventually, we came across a man sitting on the corner of the sidewalk and, after saying good evening and describing Nesta, we asked if he'd seen him.

'You mean young Marley?' he asked, glancing behind him. 'He was here just a while ago.'

Just then I heard the noise of children playing nearby, and I went to look and spotted Nesta romping among them on the street-corner.

'Nesta!' I cried.

He jerked up and looked around quickly. 'Mamma!' he squealed, shooting out from among his playmates and darting across the street to throw his arms around my waist. 'What a way you fat, eh?' he cried with delight, giving me a squeezing hug.

We stood in the middle of the street, kissing and hugging in front of all the gawking bystanders and passers-by. Then he took me to the woman at whose house he had been living, leading me through the back lanes and winding footpaths of the neighborhood to the bungalow where we found Miss Gray, sitting on her small verandah, trying to cool off in the shadows of the late afternoon.

Miss Gray turned out to be an old woman who was almost completely bald and whose trembling hands were shriveled and cracked with an unhealthy dryness. I introduced myself to her, wondering what she was doing with my son who was supposed to be at boarding school in St Thomas, and she explained to me in a quavering voice that she was sick with diabetes, could hardly walk, and that Captain had brought Nesta and left him to take care of her.

'You know,' she said in a quaking voice, 'I wondered why you never come to look for your son. And I wondered why Captain never come back to see de boy after leaving him with me. But I was glad for de help. Without Nesta, I can't even get food from de market, for I just can't get around any more.'

She added that she had no family left in the world and had never had any children of her own, and that if Nesta could only stay and look after her, upon her passing she would gladly will him all her worldly goods.

'I'm sorry, Miss Gray,' I said firmly but gently, for my heart went out to this abandoned old woman, 'but Nesta is coming home with me to de country dis very evening. Nesta,' I told him, 'go and collect your belongings.'

With a lively scampering, Nesta disappeared into the small little house to pack.

'I let him go to school,' Miss Gray mumbled lamely. 'But I don't have nobody else. He is all of life to me.'

'He is my joy to hold and to have, Ma'am,' I said, trying to stay calm. 'His father told me he was in St Thomas at boarding school. I thank you for de time you kept him here, for he is looking very nice and fat, and it shows you were caring for him.'

Nesta came out of the house with a small grip crammed full of his clothes, and we said goodbye to Miss Gray, who shrank down in her chair like she had just been beaten.

'I don't know what goin' happen to me now,' she whispered, as we left her alone in the gathering shadows of her tiny verandah.

That evening we went to my brother Solomon's house in Jones Town, where we spent the night. I asked Solomon to recommend a barber and took Nesta to the shop for a haircut. Then Nesta and I walked down to Parade in Kingston, where I bought him a new brown suit from a street vendor.

Delighted at being reunited with his family, Nesta kept calling my brother 'Uncle Solla! Uncle Solla!' like he was overjoyed just to be able to call someone 'Uncle'. He ran up and down squealing with innocent happiness and romped with his three boy cousins in the yard like a little dog who was seeing his mistress again after a long absence.

That night when Nesta was asleep, I went and stood over his bed and marveled to myself, 'What a handsome little boy dis!' for in the dimness of the room, he was a beautiful child who filled my heart with pride.

The next day we returned to Nine Miles, and I re-enrolled Nesta in the Stepney school. As she had predicted, Teacher Isaacs said that Nesta had come back not as bright as he had been when he had left, which she said was due to the poorer schooling of Kingston. I just bit my tongue and didn't tell her what had really happened.

After his return home, Nesta lost weight and began to look drawn and thin. Teacher Isaacs noticed the change in him and suggested that I buy goat's milk from Teacher James, who kept a herd of goats in the mountains, and give it to Nesta to drink every day, which I did, and the milk soon restored him to his natural, healthy look.

As for my so-called husband, I immediately wrote him a letter, telling him that I had found out about all his lies and liberated Nesta from Miss Gray's clutches. Many years later, I learned that after taking Nesta from Nine Miles, Captain had stopped off at the nearby district of Sterling, where he'd spent a week with some white friends, and where Nesta, along with a playmate he'd met there, was photographed on the knee of a woman (see first picture section).

Captain never answered the letter that I wrote blasting him for allowing our son to be used by some strange old lady as her errand boy. And I never found out what his connection was to poor sick Miss Gray.

The years ran through. Nesta thrived and grew and lived happily among his family of loved ones, establishing a special closeness with Puppa, his grandfather Omeriah.

Meanwhile, I heard nothing from Captain. He sent no money to support his son. He wrote me no letters. It was like he had flown away to the moon. I knew he was in Kingston, but I didn't know where. Plus, he was white, and I was black, and I couldn't just go and knock on his gate even if I knew where he lived, for I was certain that his family would run me.

So years and years rolled past, and I heard nothing from Captain, and Nesta had no dealings with his natural father. Then one day my sister received a letter from my Aunt Ivy, who said that she had recently seen Captain in the company of a white woman on Waltham Park Road in Kingston. The letter said that the woman who was with Captain had come to ask Aunt Ivy about renting her garage to expand a private school.

Making up my mind to investigate, I took the bus to Kingston and set out to ask for Captain at every private school on Waltham Park Road. I knocked at the gate of school after school, asking if this was Mrs Marley's school, only to be told 'No.' Eventually, a woman at one of the schools told me where Mrs Marley could be found, and I immediately went to the address and knocked at the gate.

A servant answered my knock.

'Good afternoon,' I said. 'Is one Mrs Marley living here, please?'

'Yes,' she replied.

'I would like to see her, please,' I said.

She opened the gate and told me to follow the walkway to a dingy garage, which was on the side of the house. Inside the small garage, whose door was half-open, I could see an old piano and the furnishings of a small school. A curtain divided the garage into two small compartments. The front of the garage was in use as a nursery school. Behind the curtain were cramped living quarters.

A fair-skinned woman of what Jamaicans call a 'high yellow' complexion emerged from behind the curtain after a few minutes and said, 'I am Mrs Marley. Can I help you?'

'Can I speak to Mr Marley, please?' I asked politely.

'Who are you?' she asked.

'My name is Davis,' I lied.

She looked long and hard at me, then went to the curtain and said, 'Captain, there is a Miss Davis here to see you.'

From the rear of the garage came Captain's voice. 'Who is it? Ciddy?' He shuffled out from behind the curtain, looking old and shrunken.

'So, Captain,' I greeted him, 'is here so you is?'

He could only stare at me, his lower lip quivering, before bursting into tears and sobbing like his heart had broken.

'All dese years you gone, eh, Captain?' I said, while the woman stood at his side, looking from me to him, fretfully knotting and unknotting her fingers.

'Dat's my husband you're wid,' I told her.

She exploded with a nervous laugh of astonishment. 'He's sick,' she said hastily. 'A motorcycle lick him down on the street. I'm here taking care of him. I'm getting no support. I have to be helping him.'

I glared at Captain. 'Don't you long to see your son, Captain?' I asked. 'Remember you took him from me and left him with Miss Gray? He's with me now.'

Captain sobbed louder while the fidgety woman looked on and wrung her hands with bewilderment. Over his sobs she would occasionally blurt, 'I have to be working hard to take care of him. I'm getting nothing from it. Nothing at all.'

'I'm going to bring Nesta to see you tomorrow evening,' I told Captain, leaving him weeping uncontrollably in the grimy garage.

The next day I returned to the garage with Nesta, who was then ten years old. We sat with Captain in the front of the garage. He kissed Nesta's hand and hugged him and began to sob again, wildly and loudly.

After hugging and kissing Nesta, bitterly weeping all the while, Captain put his hands into his pocket and pressed something into Nesta's hand. It was two copper pennies.

Sitting in that garage, watching Captain weeping and hugging our son, I felt sick.

That was the last time Nesta would ever see his father.

When I returned to Nine Miles, I immediately went to the police station in Alexandria and filed a charge against Captain for bigamy. A few months later I was subpoenaed to appear in court along with two of my uncles who had witnessed my marriage on Yaya's verandah.

Captain appeared in the small courthouse with his high-yellow woman friend and his nephew Cecil serving as his lawyer. I had no lawyer on my side, for I had never been to court before and didn't know what to do.

All the people who had business in court that day gathered on a small porch, waiting for their case to be called. Captain stood there among the other litigants, looking old and shaky. One woman exclaimed on seeing him, 'Who dis white man, eh? Him eye blue like de Carib Sea!'

When our names were called, we shuffled inside the courthouse and stood before the judge. To this day, I don't know what happened next. All I know is that Captain's nephew spoke to the judge, who asked Captain, 'How many times have you been married?'

'I only remember I married one time,' Captain babbled in a confused, shaky, old man's voice. 'I don't remember anything else these days. One time is all I remember. And I remember that I have a son.'

The judge said something else and rapped the gavel, dismissing the case. Later, I found out that the charges had been dismissed on the grounds that Captain was senile.

We found ourselves outside the courtroom in a crowded hallway, where I asked a nearby constable what had happened.

'You should have put a lawyer on you case,' he replied.

'I didn't want no lawyer,' I snapped. 'All I wanted was dat he free me name from his own.'

After that day in court I saw the new so-called Mrs Marley one more time. I had moved from Nine Miles to St Joseph Road, off Waltham Park Road in Kingston, and one Saturday I met her on the street. I crossed the road and accosted her. 'Tell me something,' I asked her bluntly, 'you not going to give my son anything out of what his father has?'

'I have to be working very hard for my bread and butter,' she protested in a shrill voice, glancing nervously around at people streaming past us in the street. 'He don't have one thing to offer me! He has nothing to call his own!'

'You mean he don't have nothing?' I pressed her. 'What happen to his lifelong earnings?'

Just then she exclaimed, 'Oh my God, I'm bleeding!'

I looked and saw blood dripping from her hands. 'But you must have a pin somewhere on you that stuck you!' I said.

'I don't know why I'm bleeding!' she cried hysterically, rubbing her hands while glancing at me with terror. 'What you do to me?'

'Cho!' I said with disgust. 'Woman, go 'way! You're a fool-fool somebody.' And I left her standing at the roadside, blubbering to herself and bleeding.

A few days later I got a letter from Cecil Marley, the lawyer in the family, warning me that if I ever again molested her, he intended to prosecute.

Later I found out about this woman. People suss-sussed that she took in the old people when they got sick and cared for them in their final days to get their worldly goods. But I never was able to find out if this was the truth or a rumor.

Some months after my encounter with the bogus Mrs Marley, I read in the obituary notices that Captain Norval Marley had died. I traveled to the records office in Spanish Town – after waiting a decent interval – and obtained an official copy of his death certificate.

I was now a widow. And Nesta was left fatherless with a birthright of two pennies.

Chapter Six

'Raise the girls and love the boys': that is how Jamaican child-rearing is sometimes described. From an early age Jamaican girls are taught responsibility – to cook, clean and sew; the boys, on the other hand, are usually just loved and let loose to romp. Today, Jamaican women are outshining their men in practically all fields, and this unequal upbringing may partly explain why.

However, that is not the way I raised Nesta: yes, he was very much loved. From the day of his birth, he was the center of attraction, his grandfather's favorite, and everyone in the district – family and friends – fussed over him. But if he was loved, he was also raised to accept responsibility and, as a child of rural Jamaica, taught early to do his share of the daily work.

From a young age, Nesta learned to wake up with the early morning birds and tramp into the misty bushland to milk the goats and cows. He helped draw water from the tank, and during times of drought when the tank ran dry, he would carry a kerosene pan down into the valley, catch water from the mountain spring, and balancing the brimming pan on his head or shoulder, lug it up the hillside trail to the house.

He learned to cook and could prepare any meal – from breakfast to dinner. He especially loved to boil fish tea and would often make it for us. And he learned to do the grocery shopping. In fact, during our life together in Kingston, Nesta was my one and only shopper. He would go to the market and buy coal for the cooking, and yam, onion, scallion, peas, breadfruit, green banana, or cho-cho for our meals. I had only to give him money on a Saturday and send him on his way. He would walk to the Carnation Market and higgle with the streetside vendors for whatever foodstuff or ground produce we needed for the week, carrying it back in a basket.

And Nesta was a lucky shopper for us, too. One time I sent him to the Chinyman's shop to buy a box of Eve Brand rice. When he returned, I opened the box and to my shock a coupon for five shillings fell out of it. At that time I was working as a maid cleaning houses for thirty shillings a week. Five shillings – one whole day's pay – was like a bountiful gift from heaven. Nesta and I were so joyful that we could have danced around the kitchen table.

Quick quick I sent him back to the shop to redeem the coupon and buy more boxes of rice in case we could find another five shillings. We didn't, but fifty-nine years later, I still remember the day Nesta brought home the box of Eve Brand rice and out of it poured five shillings' worth of Jah's desperately needed blessing.

From the moment he drew his first breath on earth, Nesta also showed a lively, adventurous spirit. I witnessed it first when he was still a toddler.

Around that time, a man from our district had mysteriously disappeared. Everybody in the district worried and speculated openly in the streets about what could have happened to him. Then one day a villager named Bobby Robb was on a hillside cutting firewood when he noticed a bunch of John Crows (Jamaican buzzards) circling the next wooded mountain peak and gave an alarm. The men climbed the hill to investigate and came across the bones of the missing villager underneath a tree from whose thick limb a rotten rope dangled.

The poor man had hanged himself. For more than a year his dead body had swung unnoticed on the bushy mountain peak.

Soon the rope frayed and broke and his bones spilled over the ground, his belt still fastened to what used to be his waist, tattered clothes still draped over his skeleton, the noose still tight in a death-grip around his neckbone.

I, along with nearly everyone in the district, climbed the hillside to see the bones, and while I was up there gawking, I happened to glance down into the commons only to see that Nesta had slipped away from whoever was watching him and was toddling all by himself through the valley trail.

I couldn't believe my eyes, and the crowd gathered on the peak, on hearing my outcry, turned from peering at the poor man's bones to marvel at the fearless infant tottering boldly from his doorstep through the green fields of his newly found world.

Nesta was never a puny-puny, crying child. Always his heart was brave and stubborn. Always he would stand his ground against anyone if he thought he was right.

One time when Nesta was only about five or six, Puppa gave him a cup of tea to drink. Nesta took one sip, made up his face and declared that the cup was dirty.

'De cup not dirty,' Puppa insisted. 'Drink it.'

'No, sah,' Nesta said. 'Me nah drink it.'

'Me say, drink it! De cup clean!' Puppa roared like a lion.

'No, sah,' Nesta said stubbornly. 'It dirty. Me nah drink outta dirty cup.'

Unable to believe his eyes and ears, Puppa, who was used to getting his way in all things, could only glare at his grandson. 'What a faisty little boy!' he finally growled, meaning that Nesta was impertinent. But in spite of his irritation, Puppa had to laugh at his young grandson's stubbornness, and eventually he gave Nesta the tea to drink in a clean cup.

Later, when we moved from Nine Miles to Kingston and Nesta would go out in the afternoons to kick the football with the rowdy boys of the neighborhood, I would warn him against keeping bad company, but he would calm me by saying, 'Don't worry, Mamma. Nobody give me orders. Nobody can ever make me do anything dat me lament over.'

I believed him. His nature was always stubborn. He would stand his ground against anyone if he thought he was right, just as he had with Puppa over the dirty cup. And as long as we lived together as mother and son, he never once got into any serious trouble because of bad company.

The life of country children in Jamaica is a hale-and-hearty, rough-and-tumble one, filled with simple joys. Their play is simple, their playthings mostly handmade.

The boys carve gigs (spinning tops) from the *lignum vitae* tree and spin them on sharpened nails driven into the sculpted wood. They make simple kites with the torn-out leaves of exercise books and coconut fronds and fly them in the mountain breezes. They nail bottle-tops to discarded broomsticks and make stick vehicles that their imaginations turn into trucks. To this day, in the countryside of Jamaica you can see a child flying down a green hillside behind a broomstick truck or chugging up a grade while making loud noises with his mouth like an overloaded vehicle straining in first gear.

Store-bought toys are not unknown, but are seldom found. More common than the real cricket bat is the one made from coconut bough. The cricket wicket was seldom, if ever, made of real wooden stumps, but usually of two piles of stones set about two feet apart. The football might be a threadbare tennis ball or a wad of last month's newspapers, but the boys still chased and kicked it as enthusiastically as if they were playing a World Cup match.

One favorite pastime of Jamaican boys is to make slingshots from the crook of a tree, discarded inner tubes, and the tongues of worn-out shoes. With this homemade weapon, the barefoot boys roam the bushland hunting birds such as grass tits, ground doves and hopping dicks. At the end of the day they fry up their kill with salt and pepper over a coal stove and sit down at a proud hunter's feast – even though half a dozen of these poor scrawny bush birds, fully cooked, barely have enough meat on them to fill an eyetooth.

All these adventures and playthings were a part of Nesta's young life as he grew into boyhood in the district of Nine Miles. He and the village boys roamed the grasslands and pastures in packs and formed lasting bonds of friendship.

One of Nesta's closest playmates during those early years was Bunny Livingston, later Bunny Wailer of Bob Marley and the Wailers. When Nesta was about six or seven years old, Bunny's father, Taddeus Livingston, who would become the father of my daughter, Pearl, built a house in Nine Miles and opened a shop. Bunny became one of the pack of village boys who, along with Nesta, romped together, walked every day to the Stepney school, and roamed the bush country of the district during times of idleness.

And these boys looked after each other. I remember, for example, that when Nesta was still very young, he developed a sore at the bottom of his foot that wouldn't heal. While roaming the bush, he had stepped on a broken bottle and cut himself, and for months and months the wound festered. No matter what I put on it, the cut still seeped with pus and looked raw.

A man in the district warned me that I should buy Nesta shoes or his toe would grow twisted up because of the way he had begun walking on the side of his foot to shield the wound on his foot-bottom. Yet nothing I tried helped it heal.

His cousin Nathan, who, at thirteen, was several years older than Nesta but one of his closest playmates, announced one evening that he knew how to cure the cut foot. He went into the fields and picked some Sybil oranges and roasted them in a coal fire. When the oranges were softened, he cut open the rind and scraped off the warm pulp, which he mixed with a smelly yellow powder called Iodiform that he had bought at the drugstore. Making a plaster of this compound, he smeared it on a cloth that he bound tightly around Nesta's foot.

Within days, the wound had scabbed over. Two weeks later, new skin had formed and the sore was completely healed.

This same Nathan was also one of the first people to make Nesta a guitar. It was a crude thing made of goat skin and bamboo and became one of the first musical instruments that Nesta ever owned and played.

For country children, the simple life brought hardship and lack. For the adults, the most grievous problem was how to make a living.

With the simplicity of country living came idleness and boredom. Night-time blotted out nearly all visible signs of life on the mountainside with a terrible darkness. Missing was the sparkle of Kingston, where the rolling hills always glitter like Christmas.

We struggled on. It was hard to make a living in the Jamaican countryparts, and I felt ashamed to go crying for support to Puppa who already had 'nuff-'nuff dependants of his own. To support me and Nesta, I tried my hand at shopkeeping in Stepney.

It was then that I began to notice that many people were dropping by the shop especially to see Nesta, who at that time was only five or six years old, and that he had begun to regularly read the palms of my waiting customers. At first I paid little attention to this, putting it down to childish showing-off, but then I began to notice that the adults were paying close attention to what Nesta was telling them as he pored over their open palms. I would wrap the flour or sugar or whatever I was selling, and watch him out of the corner of my eye, smiling to myself at this, his latest plaything.

But one day a woman named Aunt Zen came to my shop

and remarked, 'You know, Auntie Ciddy, Nesta can really read hands.'

'He's just playing,' I replied.

'No!' she said firmly. 'Auntie Ciddy, everything Nesta tell me come true!'

'How can that be?' I asked, doubting.

'I don't know, Auntie Ciddy,' she said, bobbing her head with certainty. 'All I know is dat child tell me nothing but de truth.'

The same opinion was seconded by a man named Solla Black, who was a District Constable in the parish and not a flighty-flighty man to run joke. He came into the shop one day and Nesta said to him, 'Make me read you hand.' Then he took Solla's hand and began to read it.

When Nesta was done, Solla came over to me, for he could see me sitting on my shopkeeper's stool laughing at Nesta's antics, and said with a serious face, 'Make me tell you something, Auntie Ciddy: every word dat dat child tell me is true. Everything he see inna me hand is true!'

'You mean it?' I asked, puzzled.

'Whether him know or not, everything him tell me is true. And is only me hand dat him read.'

I didn't know what to think, but I knew Solla was respected throughout the district as a serious man who was nobody's fool.

But just as quickly as this phase developed, it soon blew over like a morning breeze. It passed while Nesta was absent from the district, having been delivered by his father into the clutches of Miss Gray. He was gone for several months. People would come into the shop and ask for him. A few would go away disappointed, muttering about wanting to get another reading.

But soon I had found Nesta and freed him from decrepit Miss Gray. I brought him back to Stepney, and he began again to help me out around the shop in the afternoons after school.

Shortly after Nesta had returned, Aunt Zen entered my shop and laid her open wrinkled hand on the counter for him to read.

Nesta just glanced at the hand; he made no move to read it. Aunt Zen impatiently tapped the counter with her knuckles. Nesta went over to her.

'I don't read hand no more,' he told her politely.

'What?' she exclaimed, picking up her hand. 'You no read hand no more?'

'No,' Nesta said. 'I sing now.'

Others have written that Nesta was born with psychic powers; some claim, for example, that Nesta put a curse on Leslie Kong of Federal Records, causing him to drop dead suddenly at thirty-eight from a heart attack. Kong was said to have exploited Nesta in producing his first recorded song, 'Judge Not'.

I don't know personally about these things, for I never interfered in Nesta's business. I only know the things I witnessed him do with my own eyes when he was a child. He used to read palms; serious-minded villagers swore that he was accurate. Then he abruptly stopped.

And, instead, he began to sing.

One other incident from these early years stands out in my memory. It happened while I was away in Kingston working as a maid and Nesta was staying at Alderton with my sister Amy.

One day after school an older boy began to chase Nesta. I don't know if they were fighting or just enjoying some rough horseplay. To escape the boy, who was hard on his heels, Nesta darted down the winding marl lane, ducked into the backyard of a house on the roadside, and nearly crashed headlong into a freshly made coffin, its lid gaping open for the body of someone in the house who had only just died. Nearby, under a tree, was the mounded dirt of a freshly dug grave. So terrified was Nesta at this sight that he raced out of the yard, tumbled, fell, and ripped open his right knee.

That day in Kingston I received a telegram telling me that my son had chopped open his knee and had been taken to the doctor in Claremont to have the cut stitched. For the rest of his life, Nesta would bear a visible scar from that wound.

When I came back to the country I asked him about what had happened. Nesta said that he had been so frightened at nearly stumbling into an open coffin in the backyard that he had tried to run away from it too fast and had tripped and tore open his knee on a stump.

Yet I sometimes wonder: with his gift of second sight, did Nesta glimpse something that day in the gaping coffin that made him fly out of that backyard in breakneck terror?

What might he have seen that day?

Chapter Seven

Times were hard for me and Nesta during those rough years in Stepney. We were living from hand to mouth, battering from pillar to post with the ramshackle shop, which was barely putting food on the table. Most of my customers wanted to trust goods. Many could not repay when they said they would. Others would pay a shilling or two a week, then want to trust another five shillings' worth of groceries.

At the time I was in partnership with a man from my district, but since we could not see eye to eye, without telling him I made arrangements on my own to rent another shop. When he found out, he came one night to my house and called out to me to come down from the kerosene-lamp glow on my doorstep into a darkened, bushy spot in the yard to discuss business. But I refused to meet him in the darkness for I knew he was vexed. Eventually, he went away grumbling in the night as he disappeared down the woodsy trail.

But this second shop was as poor as the first – everything trust-trust, with little-little actual selling: a pound of sugar; two pounds of flour; half a pound of saltfish; a bar of soap; two cigarettes; half a dozen eggs; and everything was, 'Put it down inna de book, Auntie Ciddy,' with the accounts mounting up so much in arrears that sometimes I didn't even have enough money to buy fresh stock.

I had to find another way to support me and Nesta.

*

I tried my hand next at higglering – transporting fruit and produce from the country to sell in Kingston. But higglering in Jamaica is not an easy life.

You pack your goods – usually ground produce such as yam, breadfruit, cocoa or plantain, or seasonal fruit such as mango or Otaheite apple or June plum – and you board a bus or truck for Kingston.

Sometimes you travel all night in the back of an overloaded truck, riding atop of whatever goods it is hauling, chock-a-block with thirty or forty other higglers for the long chilly drive in the pitch-darkness down the winding mountain road to the lighted plains of Kingston. You grab what little sleep you can over the grating of the truck's gears and the whine of its engine, your head bouncing against a bunch of bananas or flapping against a stack of motorcar tires – whatever the truck happens to be hauling – pulling into sleeping Kingston at dawn light, with red eyes, throbbing shoulders and aching bones. Sometimes you get there before the market is open and you unfurl a piece of cardboard on to the sidewalk pavement and catch an hour or so of restless sleep before a blast of tropical sun threatens to bake you in a pie on the concrete.

But my first and last try at higglering was a dismal flop: the Kingston boys robbed me of every penny. I fell victim to market 'bores', thieves who work in groups, one distracting you while the other 'bears' off your goods to a nearby accomplice. Their favorite target is someone like me – a new higgler from the country who is unschooled in their thieving ways.

They surrounded me, all pretending to want to buy at the same time, and while I was trying to deal with them, someone shied a lime that hit me hard on the shoulder. I looked around but could spot no thrower. Meanwhile, a nearby higgler – one of those strapping battle-axe women whose barrel-belly was wrapped in a big-pocket apron – began to rant and rave about hooligans throwing things in the market. She carried on so loudly and violently that I finally said to her, 'Den, why you have to vex? Is me de lime catch and me not fussing.'

After the crowd of thieves had melted away from around my basket, the ranting higgler woman waddled up to me and growled, 'If I was your husband, I'd beat your ass.'

Astonished, I looked at her and asked, 'Why you say dat?'

She said impatiently, 'De lime dat lick you, is me throw it, you know! I was trying to sign you off. You know how much piece of yam pass off here and gone? You know how much dem boys thief from you?'

Checking my goods spread out on the cement floor around my basket, I discovered that she was right – much of it was gone: hands of bananas, heads of yam, bunches of guineps, had all disappeared.

I felt so downhearted I just sold off everything that was left as cheaply and quickly as I could and, with my tail between my legs, boarded the bus back to the country.

That night, before I reached back to Nine Miles, even Puppa had heard about how the bores had robbed foolish me in the Kingston market. Nesta tried to comfort me, but I still felt humiliated and ashamed at my denseness. It was obvious to me that if I had any talent, it was not for higglering.

I gave it up for good.

But there was still the problem of making a living, of providing for me and my growing son and removing us as another burden on Puppa's shoulders. I cast around for something to do for a living.

Around this time my brother John came to visit Nine Miles from Kingston and told me that his wife was leaving for England to study nursing. He asked me if I'd like to come to Kingston and keep house for him.

I discussed the offer with Puppa and he said it might be a good idea for me to get a fresh start in Kingston. So leaving

Nesta with Puppa and my sister Enid in the house that Captain had had built for me and Nesta, I moved to Kingston to live with brother John.

Kingston was a glittery city, and to my innocent country eyes seemed to sparkle with magic at night, but life there was not easy for a poor woman by herself.

I found a job as a live-in maid in St Andrew, where the well-off white and brown Jamaicans resided. I lived in the servant quarters of the house, working six days a week cooking, cleaning, ironing, washing, from early morning to late at night when the family finally went to bed. The work was not easy, the hours long, the chores wearisome. But because I was also getting room and board, I was able to save my money and send things to Nesta in the country.

In the ensuing months, I went from one job to another, trying live-in work as well as day work. One couple I worked for lived together like puss and dog, always fussing and fighting with one another. Many Fridays the husband would disappear on a night-time spree to some rum bar, leaving the wife stranded at home, weeping. When I would come to collect my pay, she would tell me tearfully that she had no money, that her husband hadn't yet brought home his pay-check. On Monday, I'd have to spend bus fare to get to their house, where I'd wait outside in the yard for the husband to arrive so I could beg him for my previous week's pay.

But at least I was working. And I was making money that I could use to help support Nesta.

Christmas came, and I returned to Nine Miles, bringing two suits and a new pair of shoes for Nesta. He had grown bigger while I was gone, but remained just as headstrong and stubborn.

I presented him with the new suits. He hurriedly dressed up in one and ran squealing up and down the street, proudly showing it off to his friends. When he came strutting back inside the house, the suit already looked worn and soiled from his gallivanting about in it.

'Listen,' I warned him, 'save de other suit for de Boxing Day garden party in Alva. You can wear it dere and look nice and clean for Christmas. Don't put on de odder suit and dirty it up.'

'Yes, Mamma,' he said, giving me a hug, for the two suits and new shoes well sweeted him.

But like any child, Nesta could not resist prancing about in his new suit. When I wasn't looking, he put it on and went romping up and down in the red dirt and the whole of the new suit got badly soiled.

Boxing Day arrived, and a pick-up was coming by to take us to the garden party in Alva. I told Nesta to wash up, put on his new clean suit, and get ready.

'Mamma,' he said in a small, guilty voice, 'de suit dirty.'

'You mean you dirty up de odder suit?' I asked. 'De one I tell you fe save for de garden party?'

He hung his head. 'Yes, Mamma.'

'Den you can't go,' I told him. 'Now, I'm all dress up. And you don't have anything nice to wear. So you can't go. Dis will learn you something – to obey what I tell you.'

He hung his head and looked disappointed.

Being a woman of a prideful spirit, I could not allow my only son to go to the garden party looking like a ragamuffin and have people suss-suss about how I couldn't even buy him proper Christmas clothes.

The pick-up arrived and, dressed in our sportiest clothes and in a happy mood of merrymaking, we all piled in, leaving Nesta behind sulking in the empty yard.

The garden party was in full swing when we arrived, the booths filled with glittering wares and games of chance, the party-goers strutting up and down in their Christmas outfits, the girls with bright ribbons in their hair, the boys in crisp, starchy suits and squeaky new shoes.

I was strolling about, enjoying the colorful booths decorated with bright streamers and paper bells and exchanging Christmas greetings with everyone when all of a sudden I thought I spotted Nesta out of the corner of my eye slinking across the grounds.

I stopped dead in my tracks and bawled out to him. He shuffled over to stand before me, hanging his head like a naughty schoolboy.

'Go right back to de yard,' I said. 'Go right back! Because I tell you you wasn't to come down here. Look how me clean. And look how you dirty! People goin' talk. Go on back to de yard!'

He looked at me and walked off with a downcast air, without arguing.

But he disobeyed me, and for the rest of the afternoon I would occasionally glimpse him among the crowd. When I approached, he would dodge me and quickly dart out of sight. When darkness was falling and it was time to go home, I spotted Nesta again among a crowd of boys, but they all ran away squealing and laughing when they saw me coming.

That night I thought about punishing him for disobedience, but I held my hand. I was living and working in Kingston. Nesta was here without me. The separation was hard on both of us.

Later that night when he thought I was asleep, he sneaked into the house and made his way quietly to his room. I was in my bed when I heard the flooring squeak from his footsteps, but I gave no sign that I was awake.

Then, after he had settled down, I tiptoed and peeked into his darkened room and saw that he appeared to be soundly sleeping, my beautiful brown angel. I just stood their quietly in the doorway, feeling a mother's joy well up in my so-proud heart, while outside the dark mountain night rang with the cries of whistling frogs and the grunting of croaking lizards.

During that quiet moment, I made up my mind that one way or another I would bring my son to live with me in Kingston.

*

But I couldn't – not just yet. I had lately moved from brother John's to the house of brother Gibson, whose lifestyle suited me better.

Like me, Gibson was sporty and fun-loving. On Friday nights he liked to go dancing and would take me along for a taste of night-life excitement, whereas brother John was a somber-minded man who worked nights at the customs office and ran like a never-late train between work and home. To me, a young girl flush with the vim and vinegar of youth, brother John's life seemed dreary and dull.

Yet until Nesta could join me in Kingston, I felt that I had to make a change in his living arrangements. I was worried that living in Nine Miles with Puppa, Nesta was missing too much school. Puppa, I knew from my own experience, was not a man to force a child to go to school, and Nesta, with his stubborn streak, would most likely prefer the freedom of skylarking in the fields and woodlands to being cooped up in a classroom miles down the road under the rule of a no-joke country teacher.

So I went to my sister Amy in Alderton and asked her if she would keep Nesta and see that he went to school. She agreed.

Packing Nesta's clothes in a grip, I took him to Alderton and left him to live under the watchful strictness of sister Amy. Puppa understood, although he was reluctant to give him up, for he said Nesta had become his very right hand.

The months rolled past. I continued working, sending money down to Nesta for his upkeep, and corresponding frequently with him. On some weekends I would take the bus to the country and visit him.

But then one day I got a message that Nesta had run away from sister Amy in Alderton, and returned to Puppa's house. My sister Amy, being childless and stern, was not a woman to brook any nonsense from a child. But, as I later found out, Nesta had run away from her to escape punishment.

A Jamaican yard is a communal dwelling-place usually occupied by more than one family, each with his own small house within a stone's throw of his neighbor's. No matter how severe the hardship, Sunday is a day when everyone eats, and often out of the same yard pot.

On this particular Sunday, the adults and their various broods had trooped off to church in their Sabbath finery, leaving Nesta and his cousin Sledger behind in charge of cooking the pot of food for the yard dinner. But having cooked the food as instructed, the two of them had also eaten up nearly the whole potful of it. When the adults returned from worship, they would be hungry and plenty-plenty vexed to find that two greedy-belly boys had gobbled down their Sunday dinner.

With Sledger at his side, Nesta hurriedly packed his things in his grip, scampered back to Nine Miles and the protection of his grandfather, Omeriah, and was now refusing to return to sister Amy.

When I found out, I made up my mind that things couldn't continue in this way: Nesta had to come and live with me in Kingston, where he would have a chance to attend secondary school. He was growing bigger every day. He needed the opportunities only Kingston could provide.

But where would we live?

Then, as I was considering my mind and fretting, like a godsend, my Aunt Ivy invited me to come and share an apartment on Beckford Street where she lived alone with her daughter. She said they had plenty of room, but the rent was a burden. I agreed, provided I could send for Nesta. She said yes, and I wrote to Puppa telling him to put Nesta on the bus.

Two weeks later, looking young, strong and handsome, Nesta stepped off the country bus at the Parade terminus. We hugged and kissed with joy at being finally reunited. Then he picked up his heavy grip with a manful effort, and the two of us set out to our new home on Beckford Street in Kingston.

Chapter Eight

The first thing I had to do was to get Nesta registered in a school, but being as none was near Beckford Street, I listed as his address the house in which brother Gibson lived with his girlfriend, Pat, and got him into the Ebenezer government school near Nelson Road. And although we lived clear down on Beckford Street, quite a distance away, Nesta went to that school for a while.

Every morning, very early, we'd catch the bus together and I'd drop Nesta off at Gibson's house. From there he would walk to the Ebenezer school while I worked cleaning various houses. Sometimes he would stay overnight with Gibson and Pat to save on bus fare, joining me at Aunt Ivy's on the weekends.

During those lean years, I took every house-cleaning job I could get. I traveled all over the parish of St Andrew and the stoosh neighborhood of Barbican looking for day work among the big-belly houses. At nights, weary down to me tailbone, I'd catch the bus down to Beckford Street, sometimes stopping by to pick up Nesta, sometimes leaving him with Gibson and riding home alone.

The months ran by; the times were tough as rockstone. But every now and again a blessing would fall from heaven, like the time I got off the bus and was walking to the house I would clean that day only to glimpse a five-shilling note crumpled up and lying on the dirty roadside.

My heart pounding fast, I glanced at it and looked quickly

around to see if anyone was watching. I could spot no one, for it was still very early morning, but just to be sure, I continued on my way and then stopped like I had just remembered something important. I scratched my head, muttered to myself, turned and retraced my steps like a woman with plenty on her mind who was confused. Carefully, I stepped past the five-shilling note while I pretended to be lost in thought, for I wanted to make sure no one would see me bend down to pick up the money. After I was sure that no one was anywhere near, I again headed towards the five-shilling note, bent down quickly and scooped it up with a prayer of thanks to Jesus. That money bought Nesta food for a whole week – rice and yam that I gave to Pat to cook for his schoolday lunch.

And occasionally the times would bring fresh trouble.

One day Nesta came home scratched and bruised with his clothes ripped up. When I asked him what had happened, he said he had gotten into a fight with another boy on the road and a drunken woman had suddenly grabbed him from behind and roared to the boy, 'Beat him ass!' He said he had struggled to get away, even trying to bite her, but she pinned his arms and back against her bosom while the other boy beat him.

'Mamma,' he said, 'me don't even know who de woman is. But she smell stink and nasty.'

'Must be some old drunkard,' I told him, wiping the cuts and bruises on his face.

But looking back, I think that even this incident and the way it happened was a blessing, because through the grace of Jah Rastafari I hadn't come by and witnessed a drunken woman holding my son on the roadside for another boy to beat. For even today I know that, without a doubt, if I had been there, death would have gone on that day.

So this dreary time went. I fell out with Aunt Ivy and moved with Nesta into another house in the same yard. But realizing that I couldn't afford the bus fare to keep Nesta in the Ebenezer school – it was six pence every day – I looked around and found a private school nearby called the Model School. The fees were five shillings a week. Bus fare alone for Nesta to attend Ebenezer school was two and sixpence a week, half of five shillings, and because he could walk back and forth to the school, which was on nearby Duke Street, we would be together every night.

I registered him at the Model school after scraping up the first week's school fee.

That was the last school Nesta would ever attend.

We battered from pillar to post, moving often during those lean-cow years, always looking for a cheaper house or a more convenient place to live. One time we shared a dwelling with Gibson and Pat; another time Nesta and I stayed together in a rented room on Regent Street.

During this time, I became friendly with Mr Taddy, Bunny Livingston's father, and he got me a job at a bar working during the days, paying two pounds ten shillings a week. But things between me and Mr Taddy never ran smoothly. He was a very jealous man, even though he was married and kept at least three other women on the side in addition to me.

Nesta was not a burden during these troublesome years. I seldom got any complaints about his behavior, and rarely had to give him a beating.

One time the headmistress at the Model school sent for me. When I went to the school I found that she had locked Nesta in a backroom all day because he'd flown into a rage and gotten into a fight with another boy.

'He was outrageous,' the headmistress complained. 'I couldn't control him. That's why I had to lock him up. He was just outrageous.'

'My son was outrageous?' I asked, hardly believing my ears.

'He was uncontrollable,' she fumed.

Nesta said afterwards that the boy had started to fight him and he was only defending himself. So I put the incident down as a schoolboy scuffle and didn't fret over it.

The only time I ever beat Nesta during these hard years was one evening when I brought him a pair of brand-new Bata shoes and he immediately wore them outside to kick the football and came back in with the soles knocked off. On top of everything else, he'd come home late, too, without telling me where he was going. When I saw how he'd ruined the brand-new pair of shoes that I'd worked so hard to buy, I flew into a temper and gave him a good strapping.

He howled for his uncle, 'Uncle Gibson! Uncle Gibson!'

Gibson came rushing into the room, begging, 'All right, Ciddy! All right! No lick him no more! No lick him no more!'

With disgust, I threw down the strap. 'Listen me, now,' I warned Nesta. 'Don't go nowhere tomorrow morning, you hear me! Nowhere! See de shoes dere you knock off de bottom just as me buy it.'

The next morning I left early and went to work. When I came back that evening Nesta had cleaned up a storage room that had been a total mess. He had shined up the kitchen.

Pat greeted me at the door, remarking in a whisper, 'Oh, Miss Ciddy, it look like de whipping last night was very good for Nesta. Look in the kitchen at all de work dat he put down in dere. He cleaned up everything lock, stock, and barrel.'

I could hardly believe my eyes at how he had transformed the house: from head to toe everything was spick and span. 'Nesta,' I called.

He came running out of his room. 'Yes, Mamma.'

'What you do?'

He smiled, shuffled nervously, and looked pleased with himself. 'I just clean up a little, Mamma.'

'A little? You clean up everything! De whole place look clean as a feather! Everything look good!'

'I sorry I mash up de shoes, Mamma,' he said, looking hangdog and repentant.

I gave him a hug and we made up.

And that was the last time I had occasion to beat Nesta, for he was growing big now, nearly thirteen, and gaining a sense of responsibility.

One time, for example, a thruppence I had left sitting on the bureau suddenly disappeared. I called Nesta and asked if he had taken it.

'Yes, Mamma,' he admitted. 'I buy a slice of sweet potato pudding with it from de woman down de street.'

'Well, dat's all right,' I said, pleased at this honesty. 'But from now on, ask me first, for I might have a special use for de money. You know everything I have is yours and for you. But don't use without asking again.'

'Yes, Mamma,' he said.

That was Nesta's nature, never to deny anything he had done; instead, he would admit the doing and face the music.

After battering around from this dwelling to that one, we finally ended up in a government house in Trench Town that had been occupied as new by my brother Solomon and his wife, Ruth. But they were getting a divorce. Ruth was moving to England, where my brother was also going to join his new woman.

Solomon contacted me and advised me that if I moved in on top of him the very night before he was due to leave, the house would automatically become mine. But he warned me that Ruth was there, too, and also planning to capture the house and turn it over to one of her sisters, who was a teacher. With these government houses, possession was truly nine-tenths of the law.

So I did as he suggested, facing a scowling Ruth, who had hoped to hand off the house to her sister. In fact, Ruth was so vexed by my moving in that she called her three sons into the drawing-room and bitterly announced to them, 'I want you to remember what you father and you Auntie do for the rest of you life.'

The boys, who were then very young, just looked from one adult to another, bewildered.

The next day Ruth and her furniture were gone, and Nesta and I were in possession of a nearly brand-new concrete house, compliments of the government, at 19 Second Street, in Trench Town. It was that same house that he would later sing about in 'No Woman No Cry':

> I remember when we used to sit
> inna government yard in Trench Town.

Yet it seemed as soon as one trouble ended another began. Mr Taddy and I were not living smoothly. There was always fussing and fighting. He was a violent man with a wicked temper and a mad jealousy.

Sometimes he didn't like the way I talked. Sometimes he didn't like the way I was dressed and would just come up to me and rip off my frock and say, 'You not going anywhere.'

One time he came into the bar and saw me having a harmless drink with a gentleman patron named Mr Williams. Mr Taddy quickly strolled over to where I was sitting and boxed the glass of beer out of my hand. When I retreated into the kitchen, he followed me and tried to push me down against the hot stove.

That was only one of many fights we had, for he was a very cruel and wicked person who always had to domineer. One time, for example, during a fight, he cut me on the hand with his knife. Blood dripping from the wound, I fled to the Denham Town police station to file a complaint against him.

Seeing me do this, Mr Taddy took the same knife and sliced open his fleshy palm. Then he burst into the station, bleeding badly, ran up to the sergeant who was behind the counter taking down my statement, and bawled, 'Sergeant, look how dis woman cut me! Me want file a complaint!'

Up to then, the sergeant had been sympathetic to my injury and had intended to send a constable to arrest Mr Taddy. But when he saw Mr Taddy also bleeding before him, he assumed that we'd wounded one another in a bloody domestic fight. Angrily, he told us both to get out of his station and go to the hospital.

And it was all because of his mad jealousy that Mr Taddy behaved so wickedly. I have noticed that when men are married, they're usually more jealous of the mistress they have on the outside than they are of the wife who's patiently sitting at home waiting for them. That was the case with Mr Taddy. He was possessive and jealous and we were constantly fighting because of it. He kept a close watch over me and was very domineering.

Unfortunately, sometimes Nesta would be caught in the middle of our fights. One Friday evening, we had the worst fight of all, and Nesta got involved.

Mr Taddy was sitting on the verandah of our house, discussing the Bible with one of his cousins from St Mary. This was a thing Mr Taddy very much loved to do – sit and read the Bible and dispute about the meaning of its passages – and he was in the middle of doing this when his brother Fitzie walked up and handed him a letter.

Mr Taddy glanced at it briefly, kissed his teeth in contempt, tore up the letter and tossed it over the verandah wall. Then he returned to his biblical disputing.

I was sitting inside when this happened, and I saw the whole thing and wondered what the letter had said and who had written it. Something warned me to leave it alone, but the devil whispered in my ear, and when the men were deep into their discussion about scripture, I sneaked around the front of the house, picked up the pieces of the letter, and returning to my bedroom, carefully put them together on my bed.

It was from one of Mr Taddy's baby-mothers, a woman named Ceciline, grumbling that he had left her alone to come and be with me, his 'dirty sweetheart', and threatening that whenever she met me on the street, it would be worse than the war that had recently broken out in the Wareika Hills between the Rastas and the English army.

When I read that letter, something just got up inside me. I went out on the verandah, meaning to confront Mr Taddy, but a voice warned me not to say anything, so I retreated into the house and held my tongue.

But then the devil whispered louder in my ear, and I abruptly threw caution to the wind and stepped out on to the verandah, clutching the patched-up letter.

I called him, 'Come here, Mr Taddy,' and he followed me aside.

'What kind o' letter is dis?' I challenged him. 'Anywhere I see dis dutty gal, I goin' bust her ass.'

'An' if you bust her ass, I bust you ass,' he snarled. He picked up a stool and lifted it up as if he would hit me.

Grabbing a thick glass tumbler that was sitting on a nearby table, I smashed it hard against his ear. The glass shattered; blood exploded from the side of his head.

When I saw the thick gobs of blood gushing, I was frightened, and my knees got weak. I ran out of the yard.

He grabbed me, spun me around and thumped me in the eye, dropping me on to the ground, and, planting his foot atop my chest, took out a knife from his pocket, and started to open it up with his teeth.

Just then a burly barmaid from across the street who'd seen the fight burst into the yard and pinned his arms from behind.

'Taddy,' she screamed, 'leave de woman! Leave de woman!'
'Run, Miss Mally,' she yelled to me. At the time, 'Miss Mally', a cross between 'Marley' and 'Malcolm', was the nickname that everyone called me.

Without shoes 'pon me foot, I tore out the yard and dashed across the street into a house owned by a woman named Miss Tilley. Peeping through the window, I watched the commotion across the street, staying carefully out of sight, for I knew that Mr Taddy's blood was so hot that in his present mood he could easily commit murder.

I saw him go to the cistern in the yard and wash the blood off his face. Realizing that I wasn't safe where I was, I waited until no one was looking, then I darted into the street and ran away from the neighborhood into the yard of an old lady every-one knew as 'Mammy'. Fitzie, Mr Taddy's brother, lived in this same yard.

When I burst into her house and blurted to an astonished Mammy what had happened, she lifted her hands and cried, 'Lawd Jesus! You draw blood?'

My knees were trembling. 'Yes, Mammy.'

'Boy,' Mammy said, 'me have fe go down dere and see what happen.'

'Yes, Mammy,' I begged her. 'Go down and see what happen, for maybe dem goin' call de police.'

Warning me to stay out of sight, she went out, carefully clos-ing the front door behind her, leaving me cowering in her drawing-room.

She was gone for what seemed like for ever, and when she returned, her face was hardened. 'Mally,' she said in a shaken voice, 'you cut him bad, you know.'

'What?' I cried. 'It bad?'

'Yes, Mally. And dem have to carry him gone a hospital.'

'Den is bad, bad, bad?' I asked, my voice trembling.

'Yes, Missis. It really bad fe true.'

While we were talking in whispers, Fitzie, Mr Taddy's brother, came into the yard, for he lived in one of the rooms, and he stepped on to the verandah and bawled to Mammy, 'Man, if you ever see what happen to Taddy! But him deserve what him get, for him have all dem whole heap a gal gal gal de fool around with and have him wife. No wonder all dem something happen to him. Big married man have all dem little old gal all over de place . . .'

I stepped from inside the room. 'Who you talking 'bout?' I asked.

Fitzie was so frightened to see me that his jaw nearly locked up. 'Miss Mally,' he stammered apologetically, 'me a tell you de truth, me no see what him do you, but me see what you do him. But every story have two side.'

'Him cut bad?' I asked.

'Yes, him cut bad. Dem gone with him up to de hospital.'

'Everything clear up down dere now?'

'Yes, Miss Mally.'

Later I learned that Nesta had come home to find Mr Taddy bleeding from his headside wound and the whole yard in a noisy uproar. Mr Taddy sent Nesta uptown to get his wife, Miss Maggie, who came down to the house to find him moaning in pain and bleeding badly.

Howling with rage, Mr Taddy screamed at his wife, 'Look what dis dirty gal do to me, Maggie! Look how she cut me! What me fe do? You think me should call de police and make dem arrest her?'

'Fe what? Fe put you name inna de newspaper?' Miss Maggie snapped. 'De best thing you can do to dat nasty gal is leave her. You better go hospital before you bleed to death.'

That night, after everything had quieted down, I reached home and found the door to my house wide open. Inside, every piece of furniture was smashed to pieces: my cabinet, my center table, anything with glass in it lay just shattered and strewn across the floor.

'What happened?' I asked a woman who was sitting in the yard, catching a peaceful late-night smoke.

'Miss Maggie mash up you house,' she said, shrugging.

Nesta, who was about fifteen years old at the time, was very angry and upset when he saw me with a black eye. 'When I grow big, Mamma, and become a man,' he vowed, touching my bruised eye, 'I goin' lick dat man back inna him eye. You wait and see.'

'No,' I said wearily, 'you don't have to do dat. You'll just bring more trouble.'

And Nesta never did.

A child grows up, takes on his own responsibilities in life and, with the eyes of a man, sees childhood episodes differently. In later life Nesta himself would occasionally have to slap up his own woman when her mouth got too 'nuff.

So after that I never heard him talk again about getting revenge against Mr Taddy.

Even though blood had flowed in this latest fight, Mr Taddy and I soon made up and continued our relationship. Eventually, he even replaced the furniture his wife had mashed up.

So we continued uneasily, fretfully, never smoothly.

Many years later, when Nesta was dying at the Issels clinic in Germany, he suddenly stirred in the dining-room of our rented house one evening, looked around and asked me, 'Mamma, you know Mr Taddy's number?'

'No,' I said, 'I don't know his number.'

He looked like he had something weighing heavily on his mind.

'You know, Mamma,' he said softly, 'I want talk to him. Dat man is me father, you know. Dat's de only man dat ever buy me a pair of shoes.'

I was quiet for a moment, then I said, 'Dat's good. Dat's good.'

He said, 'I going call Diane and ask her to pick him up and carry him to Hope Road so I can talk to him.'

So Nesta phoned Diane Jobson, his attorney and close friend in Jamaica, and she did as he asked: she went to Mr Taddy's house and brought him around to 56 Hope Road, which is now a museum, where he could phone Nesta in Germany.

The phone rang; Nesta answered, and I overheard their conversation.

'A you dis?' Mr Taddy exclaimed, excited. 'Everybody up here say you dead, man.'

'Yeah, well, so dem say,' Nesta replied wearily, for he was then on death's own doorstep.

'Boy, me can't get over dis,' Mr Taddy gushed, ''cause me can't believe a you me a talk to.'

The two of them chatted for a while about old times. 'How everything wid you?' Nesta asked, at which Mr Taddy launched into a recital about how times were rough and how hardship was upon him.

'All right,' Nesta said quietly, 'I goin' send something for you.'

'Thank you,' Mr Taddy said. 'Take care o' yourself, Nesta. God bless you.'

After the conversation was over, I asked Nesta, 'How much are you going to give Mr Taddy?'

He looked up. 'Thirty thousand dollars,' he said.

I thought then to myself that Nesta shouldn't give Mr Taddy the whole thirty thousand. He should give Mr Taddy twenty thousand and give my brother John ten. But I didn't open my mouth with any opposition.

As it turned out, Mr Taddy didn't get a penny of this money.

The check had to be signed by both Nesta's wife, Rita, who was on and off in Germany, and Diane Jobson, who was then in Jamaica, and before the two of them could get together to sign the check, Nesta had passed.

And Mr Taddy got nothing.

Chapter Nine

Nesta was now a teenager with his own life. I was working at the bar, and he was attending the Model school. He had his own little ups and downs and, like any teenage boy, was away a good part of the time, gallivanting about town with his friends. He had become caught up in the rough and tumble life of Kingston's mean streets, and every now and again something would happen to him that would scare me half to death.

One afternoon, for example, a tough-looking street boy swaggered into the bar and said nonchalantly to me, 'Lady, you have a son named Nesta?'

'Yes,' I said, my heart leaping into my throat.

'He got a chop over his eye.'

'What? Where is he?' I stammered.

'He down at de school,' the boy said indifferently. Then he wandered out of the bar as if all he'd said was a civil 'Good afternoon.'

Frantic, I asked Mr Anderson, my neighbor who had a shop next door, to keep an eye on the bar, telling him that my son was hurt and I had to go to him. Then I raced out into the hot, dirty streets of Kingston to find Nesta.

I ran down to the school and found some ragged street boys perched on a wall surrounding the school-yard. When they saw me coming, one of them cried, 'Babylon!' which, then and now, is the nickname Jamaicans use for the police or authority. At this, most of the boys scattered like wild birds over the wall and flew into the buildings of the school. One of them, however, just slouched against the wall and eyed me cockily.

'You know a boy name Nesta Marley?' I asked him.

'Me don't know anybody name dat,' he mumbled sullenly.

I didn't believe him, so I nosed my way around the stained back of the school building, only to glimpse Nesta among the pack of boys, who scampered off when they saw me coming. I couldn't catch up with them, so I returned to the bar, telling myself that Nesta couldn't be badly hurt or he wouldn't have run away.

Later on he came to the bar and stood outside on the sidewalk, too ashamed to enter. Glimpsing him, I rushed out into the street.

'What you doing out here?' I asked him. 'Come here! Make me see de cut.'

He came over hesitantly and showed me a band-aid plastered over his eye.

'What happened?' I asked, examining the wound.

He said that one of his friends had thrown a stone and chopped him over his eye, but that it had been an accident.

'So why you run from me, den?' I challenged.

'Because, Mamma,' he said, 'me think you'd get vex when you see me head bleed and call police 'pon de boy. And him no mean to do it.'

I said, 'Oh.' It was all I could think of to say.

The gash from the stone had missed his eye by about two inches. But when you lived among the wanton wickedness of Kingston, you learned to be thankful for all Jah's mercies, no matter how small or accidental.

One evening Nesta came home from school singing a song:

> *I went in the garden alone,*
> *while the dew was still on the roses,*
> *and the voice I heard linger in my ear . . .*

I was stunned at how well he sang. Of course, Nesta had always been a singing child, even when we were living in Stepney, but this was the first time I can remember being struck by his beautiful singing voice.

I called out to him, 'You know, Nesta, dat song is very nice.'

'You like it, Mamma?' he asked, pleased at my response.

Then he sat in the small drawing-room and sang the entire song for me and me alone, the first time he had ever done that. He was then about fourteen years old. He said it was a Pat Boone song he'd heard on the radio.

When he was finished giving me a private concert, I could only marvel, 'My goodness gracious, Nesta!'

Looking pleased, he gave me a big smile and strolled into his bedroom, humming.

One evening when he was about fifteen, Nesta came home from school lugging a big pile of textbooks. Usually when he returned home from school, he would carry only one book for homework, or be empty-handed.

'What happen?' I asked him. 'Why you carry home all you books?'

'Mamma,' he said, 'de school close down. De headmistress tell us dat she going back to de country. She lock up everything.' He said he'd brought the books home to give to a friend who was still attending school.

I sighed. 'All right, now, den,' I said, 'if dat be de case, we have to go find a trade for you.'

He said yes, and then he went up to his bedroom to strum his guitar, leaving me wondering what would become of him now.

After that, he began to take his music seriously. I would hear him in his bedroom, strumming and practicing. Sometimes Desmond Dekker would come over and the two of them would start jamming together in the bedroom, making the small house ring with joyful song. Often, Nesta would go over to Bunny Livingston's house, and they would practice there. I would also hear them rehearsing at Mr Taddy's house.

Nesta began to get little gigs in the bars around town, and he and Bunny and others would sometimes team up and play as a small band. They would practice before and after a session, helping each other master a tune or play it better.

Much of this rehearsing and playing took place on the fringes of my own busy life, which was still taken up with trying to earn bread and butter for me and Nesta and keep a roof over our heads. Near the bar where I worked, I had bought a little restaurant from an Indian woman and put my sister Rose (we have the same father) to run it for me. And for a while, the little restaurant prospered. Being in the bar business, I was also meeting a lot of people daily, and I would sometimes tell them about my son who was looking to learn a trade and ask their advice. One day a man informed me about a welding business on South Camp Road that took in apprentices and taught them the trade of welding. I hurried home that evening and told Nesta, and he went to the place the next day and got on as an apprentice welder.

On the side, he continued doing his music business with Bunny, and sometimes he would help me in the restaurant. One morning I told him to open up and sweep up until I came, and he left early to do it. A little while later as I was on my way to join him, I spied him across the crowded street. He was hurrying in the opposite direction from the restaurant.

'Nesta, what happen?' I called to him across the jam-packed Kingston street.

'Mamma,' he said breathlessly, darting across the street, dodging the smoky, noisy traffic, 'dem broke de restaurant.'

We went and made a report to the police, and a constable came to inspect the premises. The lock on the back door had been ripped off. Inside, all the beer and cigarettes and soft drinks were gone. Everything that could be moved was missing.

I was so upset and vexed to see all my hard work go down the drain that I swore to sleep in the restaurant that night to personally protect my property. Nesta offered to stay the night with me, so I carried pillows and bedding to the restaurant and, after we had served the last customer and closed for the night, I made up two places for us to sleep on the floor under the counter.

As Nesta and I were settling down for the night, a friend of mine peered in through the window and gaped with amazement at the sight of me and Nesta huddling under the counter, trying to get comfortable. She rapped on the window to be admitted. I unlocked the door and let her in.

'Miss Mally,' she asked, looking horror-stricken as she entered the dimly lit shop, 'what you goin' do, sleep here?'

'Yes,' I said angrily. 'Dey not going break my restaurant dat I work so hard to keep up and thief out all my goods just like dat.'

'Miss Mally, you crazy? If thief broke inna you place tonight and you and Nesta are here, wha' you think dem goin' do? Kill you and you one pickney! Dat's wha' dem will do! Kill you!'

With a sinking heart, I realized that she was right. What I was doing was not just reckless: given the known viciousness of Kingston thieves, it was stupid.

'No, Miss Mally,' she counseled, 'you leave de little place and carry you one pickney home.'

Nesta, meanwhile, was crouched on the bedding spread out under the counter, peering up at us intently, listening to every word. I glanced down at him and sighed.

'Come, Nesta,' I said heavily. 'Come, make we lock up and leave it. Money not worth life.'

And the next week, even though I had changed the lock and barred the windows, the thieves again broke into the restaurant and cleaned me out. Downhearted, I sold the little restaurant to my brother John, who planned to avoid break-ins by staying open all night.

It seemed that no matter what little thing I tried to help myself, Kingston and its wicked ways were just determined to humbug up my life.

We went on.

Every morning, I packed a little lunch for Nesta and he left early to learn the welder's trade. After he was gone, I'd get ready and head for my own job working behind the counter of the bar.

Nesta would usually reach home before I did in the evenings. Sometimes he would cook dinner for both of us and leave a plate for me on the stove. Sometimes he would be away playing a gig at some club, and I would arrive late at night to an empty house, or to find Mr Taddy waiting in the drawing-room for my company. But no matter where Nesta was playing, every night would eventually find him home in his own bed.

At the bar, I began to hear encouraging words about Nesta and his music. One evening a man named Derek Morgan came in to have a drink. He was then active in the ska music scene in Kingston, and after he learned who I was, he said to me, 'You know, lady, you have a son who's very talented.'

'Oh yes?' I said.

'He has a lot of potential,' he said, wiping his mouth.

I thanked him for his words of encouragement and praise. Similar remarks would sometimes come my way from the night-life people who would occasionally drift into the little bar.

Nesta was still doing the music only on the side, and concentrating on learning to be a welder, which seemed to be a more practical and steady line of work. But one evening he came home in pain, complaining of something in his eye. Apparently that day there hadn't been enough goggles at the plant for all the apprentices, and he had tried welding without any eye-protection. Something sharp had flown up from the shower of welding sparks and pierced his eye. He begged me to try and get it out.

I sat him down on a chair next to a lamp, leaned his head back and, peeling his eyelids wide open with my fingers, peered into his eye. I could see something stuck in the white of his eye, but when I brushed at it with a ball of cotton, it wouldn't move.

'You see it, Mamma?' he asked, wincing.

'Yes, but it nah move when me touch it.'

'Try again. It pain me bad.'

I tried, but it was no use. Whatever he had in his eye had punctured the white jelly, where it lay deeply buried. He said that some men at the welding plant had told him to put a cold towel on it, which I did, and he went into his bedroom and stayed there in the darkness because the injured eye couldn't stand any light. All night from early evening he was in his room, and sometimes I could hear him moaning softly. Eventually, he fell asleep.

The next morning I took him to the hospital where a doctor worked on his eye and removed a piece of a metal splinter. But he told us that a piece was still left in the eye and we should come back tomorrow. The nurse put a patch over the eye and sent us home to return the next day.

Nesta was still in pain. I made him dinner and gave him some bush tea to drink, and he had another restless night. Before I went to sleep, I went in to check on him and found him abed with a pillow draped over his face, shielding his hurt eye from the street light shining through the window. I sat on the edge of his bed and asked him how he felt.

'You know, Mamma,' he stirred, 'you see dis now? If I was singing instead of welding, none of dis would happen.'

The next day my brother Gibson went with Nesta to the hospital, and the doctor removed the remaining sliver of metal embedded in the eye-white, gave him some drops and sent him home.

After that episode, Nesta wanted nothing more to do with welding.

So Nesta had no trade. He had no job. And he seemed to have no prospects. All he had were occasional gigs playing music.

Then one Saturday morning a prosperous-looking Chinyman suddenly appeared at our doorstep, asking for Nesta.

'Him not here now,' I told him.

'You know when he'll be back? I want to give him a contract.'

'Oh yes,' I said, 'a contract for what?'

'For his music,' he replied.

'Oh!' I said, getting all excited. 'Oh!'

But Nesta wasn't there, and the man soon drove away in his fine motorcar.

When Nesta returned that evening, he had already met the man on the street, signed the contract and been paid five pounds for the rights to the song 'Judge Not', which was the first song he wrote and recorded. This was also the first big money Nesta ever got for a recorded work.

In the joy and jubilation of that night, Nesta was generous with the five pounds he'd been paid for the song. He gave me two pounds out of it. To my sister Enid, who was living with us at the time, he gave ten shillings. To another woman also named Enid, who was staying with us from the country, he gave five shillings. Out of the five pounds, he kept only two pounds five shillings for himself. But that was Nesta: he gave with the heart, and he always made sure that his Mamma got her cut.

Soon after that, we would occasionally hear the song 'Judge Not' playing over the radio, and my heart would swell with pride that it had been written and performed by my one son. But I had my misgivings about the music world. And I shared them with Nesta. What I especially worried about was that the business Nesta was now involved in was one known for its appeal to the 'batty-man', which is the Jamaican patois word for men who crave the rear-parts of other men over God-given woman flesh.

I told Nesta that in the dingy little bar where I worked, I myself had seen these well-dressed brown, high-yellow and white men of posh St Andrew neighborhoods where I had once cleaned houses come prowling around at night, hunting for men and boys. Only last week, I told him, one of these same well-dressed white strangers had stumbled into the bar drunk and began buying rounds for all the hangers-on and boys, befriending them and chatting them up with sweet mouth. That same man probably had his faithful wife sitting at home in the belly of a big St Andrew house, waiting for him to come to her bed, and here he was roaming the stained back alleys and lanes of downtown Kingston, sniffing among the bad light of rat-trap bars for other men.

The next day one of the boys who had departed with the stranger returned to the bar and said, 'Miss Mally, you see dat man who was here last night? You know what him is? Him is a batty-man. Is batty him was looking.'

'What you say to me?' I exclaimed, unable to believe my ears, unwilling to imagine that such a well-dressed gentleman could be on a mission of such nastiness.

Nesta heard me out patiently. Then he said, 'Don't worry, Mamma. Nobody can make me do anything me don't want to.'

I said, yes, yes, that was true, and tried to calm my fears. But deep inside my heart, I still fretted.

I continued working in the bar and going along with Mr Taddy, even though we were still periodically fussing and fighting over his attempts to domineer. Eventually, I got pregnant for him, and he eased off a bit with the constant bullyriding. In fact, I'm now quite certain that had I not got pregnant for Mr Taddy and borne him a child – our daughter Pearl – sooner or later he would have murdered me. But once he saw me swollen with his child, his bullying attitude changed and his harsh manner softened.

Pearl was born, and I brought her home for Mr Taddy to go 'kitchy-coo' at and play with in the crib like a doting father. But I was still not happy under his rough rule.

Nesta was making his way in the world, and he was getting a name for himself. He was gone a lot on his music business, but he was still laying his head at home every night.

As for me, I was not content with my life. I wanted better. Mr Taddy's rule, even though we had a newborn infant now between us, was still an oppression.

So I did what I have always done in times of trouble: I got down on my knees and began a mighty praying every night for deliverance out of Babylon. Prayer had always been my constant staff. Night after night I got down on bended knee and told Jesus that if He would help me out of my predicament, I would serve Him as long as He gave me breath to draw. God heard my prayer and answered it.

I found out one day that my sister Ivy in Delaware had written a letter to her niece, Nola, inviting her to come to America on a visit. I quickly wrote sister Ivy and beseeched her to invite me, too. She did, and I got a visa to visit her in Delaware.

Mr Taddy was against my going, but I told him it was only for a visit, and that Enid would take care of Pearl, who was then ten months old, and eventually he gave in grudgingly. So it came that just as Nesta was breaking into the music business, I broke out of the clutches of Mr Taddy and headed for America.

Shortly after I left, Enid decided she wanted to return to Nine Miles, so Mr Taddy moved in on top of her like I had done with Ruth and took possession of the Trench Town government house. Enid took Pearl and moved back to Nine Miles. Mr Taddy brought Ceciline, the baby-mother whose letter had sparked the fight between us, to live with him in the government house, where Nesta continued to stay occasionally.

By then I was long gone and struggling to make a life in America.

Chapter Ten

I arrived in America in 1962 to a land of wealth and plenty where all was prosperous and flourishing. My Jamaican eyes were dazzled by the sights of its richness.

I stayed with my sister Ivy and her husband, a church-going gentleman everyone knew as Bishop Brown, and the marvels I saw daily were wonders to behold. One Saturday, for example, my sister and her husband went to the market and returned home with baskets of eggs – just like that – baskets and baskets of eggs they'd bought wholesale. Everything was cheap, plentiful, and readily available, even eggs that were so scarce and dear in Jamaica. Everyone in the street was well dressed and sporty and seemed rich and pleasant, even though I found their speech hard to understand.

I had come in the middle of a Delaware winter, where the outside world wore a dreariness my eyes had never before witnessed, and the wind had a bite that curdled my blood, but none of this mattered. Here, stretched out as far as the eye could see, were opportunity and prosperity. I buckled down to work hard for my share.

Bishop Brown knew some well-off people who owned a store, and he went to see the gentleman and asked if his wife needed help around the house. The man phoned his wife, who said she would welcome good household help, and in a blink I had a job paying what seemed to me a fabulous sum of money – $40 per week – helping the woman care for her house and three children.

Determined to make my way, I toiled long, hard hours like a humble beast of burden without break or rest, giving no argument or back-chat, eagerly doing all I was told, dumbly obeying my mistress's every word.

During this time, I would occasionally get news from Jamaica about Nesta. Sister Enid wrote me to say that Nesta had turned Rasta and she was afraid that the bad company he had lately been keeping would one day murder him.

In those days Rastas were feared in Jamaica. Not understanding the peaceful philosophy of the brethren, people thought them ferocious and wicked. I myself had been scared to meet them in the street with their fierce-looking dreadlocks that made them seem like wild beasts. I immediately wrote Nesta warning him to watch his step with the Rastas, but he did not answer my letter.

I had left Nesta in the Trench Town house, and soon after my departure, Mr Taddy, his baby-mother, Ceciline, and her brother, Mr Hugh, also moved in with him. In fact, for a while Mr Taddy looked after Nesta like a father. For example, one time Nesta got into a fight with another boy. The quarrel was sparked off by the boy's sister, who used to like Nesta and was hurt when he paid her no mind. This girl spread tales about Nesta, and her brother came and started fighting him. As they fought, Nesta was thrown against a barbwire fence, cutting him so deeply that he carried the scar to the grave. Mr Taddy tore into the yard, waving his machete, and ran the boy off. Later, some of Nesta's friends would back up the boy and give him such a good beating that he would put his tail between his legs and come apologize to Nesta.

So at first and in his own fashion, Mr Taddy did look out for Nesta. But that did not last long, and soon Nesta also left the Trench Town house.

It turned out that in the evenings Ceciline used to leave food on the stove-top for Nesta, Mr Taddy having taken up the responsibility of feeding him. One evening Nesta came to the house and sat down to eat some food that he thought had been set out on top of the stove for him and Ceciline had said sullenly, 'What you eating de food for? It no leave dere for you. Is for Mr Taddy.' Shamed, Nesta muttered that he was sorry and immediately rushed to the sink to spit out a mouthful of partly chewed food.

Boy and man, Nesta had always had a sense of pride, and the incident made him feel so small and hurt that from then on he kept away from the Second Street house and began staying with Bunny in Trench Town or with Coxson Dodd, who would later produce some of his music.

I got all this news second-hand, for I was then deeply involved in my own struggle to make it in America. The months had run past, and soon my temporary visitor's visa was up and I would have to return to Jamaica. Bishop Brown and sister Ivy took me to a lawyer and got me an extension, but it was clear that unless I could change my visa, my days in America were numbered. The only way for me to get my permanent papers, said Ivy, was to marry an American citizen. But who? I knew no marrying men. Who could I get to marry me?

One evening we sat around in the living-room, thinking. Bishop Brown said he knew a decent, intelligent, church-going man named Mr Booker who was divorced, and suggested that maybe I could marry him. Bishop Brown said he had worked with Mr Booker in flea markets and had always found him an upright and pleasant gentleman.

'What's his phone number?' I asked eagerly.

Bishop said he didn't know but he knew the number of Mr Booker's mother, and at my urging he immediately called, only to find that Mr Booker had just left her house and was on his way home.

'Give him ten minutes and you can call him at home,' the mother suggested.

I gave him the ten minutes. Then I called him at home, told him who I was, and asked if we could meet to discuss something important. He said he'd be right over, and true to his word, fifteen minutes later he arrived, a pleasant-looking, well-spoken gentleman fifteen years my senior.

After some initial greetings and pleasantries, we went into the living-room, where I sat with my sister's baby in my lap and put my case to him bluntly. I told him frankly that I was looking for a mature, church-going man to marry so I could get my papers and remain in America, and asked him if, through his dealings with the flock in the church, he could think of anyone who fitted that description.

Mr Booker chuckled heartily at my frankness. 'Oh no, Ma'am, no, Ma'am,' he said. 'If it's anything like that, it would have to be me.'

And it was him. Over the next few weeks, we saw each other often, and I continued to pressure him to marry me, even sometimes annoying him to the point where he would grumble that he didn't like to be pushed.

For the truth is, I was pushing him. I pushed him hard, hard. And eventually he broke down and took me to meet the sister he lived with, whose name was Elise.

One day we drove down to Dover. We had with us Edith, who was divorced from Mr Booker's brother, and Elise's boyfriend, whom everybody called Stalks. Both of them thought we were going on a weekend outing and were surprised when Mr Booker drove straight to the Records Office in Dover, telling them that he had brought them here to witness our marriage.

But we couldn't get married that day because it was a Saturday. However, we did get married the following Monday, 14 October 1963.

When we emerged from the Marriage Office that Monday as man and wife after a makeshift ceremony witnessed by two strangers and performed with a ring briefly borrowed from the

Right: My first husband, Bob's father, Captain Norval St Clair Marley

Below: My father, Omeriah Malcolm

Above: My eldest brother,
Clarence Malcolm

Below: My sisters: (from left to right) Ivy, myself,
Enid (seated) and Amy, in Wilmington, Delaware

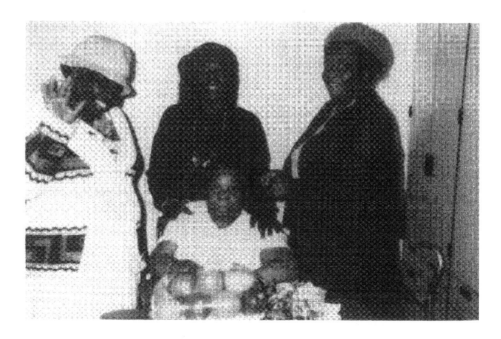

Above: Bob (right) pictured in 1949 with a playmate on the knee of a woman then unknown to me. This was in Sterling, St Ann's, after Captain Marley had taken him there for a week

Right: Bob's half-sister, Constance. Her father was Captain Marley

Left: Me in 1960. This photograph was taken in Kingston, before the birth of my daughter Pearl

Below: Bob, Pearl and myself on Second Street in Trench Town, Kingston

Right: Rita in her wedding dress

Below: Peter Tosh, Rita and Bob in Jamaica (unknown child in front)

Left: Bob, Anthony and myself in the back yard of my house in Wilmington

Below: Bob, Rita and myself in Wilmington

Right: Mr Booker with Richard and Pearl

Right below: With my children Richard and Anthony in Wilmington

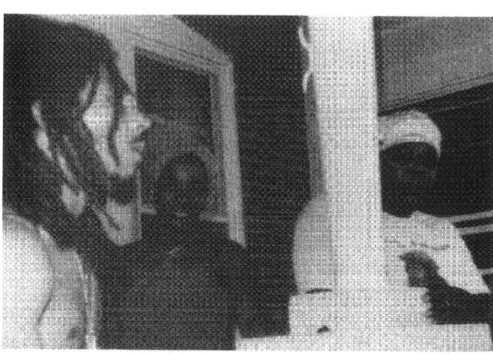

Above: With Bob in my kitchen in Wilmington, 1974

Left: Pearl, Anthony, myself and Richard

minister's wife, I felt like all earth's sunshine was glowing inside my heart. I had married an American citizen; I could now get my papers. But it turned out, too, that I now had at my side the most wonderful man to ever walk the race of Jah's earthly kingdom, and for our thirteen years together as man and wife, we shared a contented, joyous domestic life during which I bore him two sons, Richard and Anthony.

Mr Booker was a man of quiet patience and peace, and during our years together, if ever a mouth was heard gnashing within our household, it would always be mine, never his. During such quarrelsome moments he would quietly disappear out the back door and retreat to his mother's. Hours later he would phone and ask, 'Has your heart come down yet?' And if it had come down, he would meekly return home, always showing a mild and pleasant disposition.

But not everyone was happy with our marriage. Edith, his former sister-in-law, had apparently secretly loved Mr Booker too, and she made some ugly phone calls to me after we were married, breathing into the mouthpiece and calling me a 'criminal'.

That was her problem, however. I was safely and legally married to Mr Booker. And I could return to Jamaica for my children, Pearl and Nesta.

By now deeply involved in his music, Nesta was still finding the Jamaican music scene a hand-to-mouth existence. He was tied up with Coxson Dodd, but their business was not flourishing. Plus I had my doubts about Dodd and his true feelings towards Nesta.

Sometime past Nesta had written and told me that this Coxson Dodd, who was handling his music, had become very important in his life. He begged me to write a mother's letter asking Dodd to be nice to my son, and I did. In that letter I told Dodd that my son spoke highly of him and looked up to him as a big brother. I explained that since Nesta had no other brothers out there to help him get along in life, I was begging him to do whatever he could to help Nesta with his music.

However, I had misunderstood: Nesta had wanted me to send the letter directly to him, not to Dodd, to whom he would have shown it at the right time. Coxson wrote me back a letter, most of which I have forgotten. But I do recall one remark he made that stuck in my craw, to the effect that for one to gain a certain standard in any field of life, one needed education. This I took to mean that he was really looking down his nose at Nesta and not respecting him as a man, all this when Coxson Dodd was not even a quarter as educated as my son, and at no time – whether this time or that time – would he ever be.

The book of life is now closed on Nesta. And the world knows who is more educated and gifted and which one it loves and admires more – Coxson Dodd or Robert Nesta Marley.

Mr Booker, being a kind, loving and generous heart, had agreed to sponsor me, Nesta and Pearl to come to America, and I returned to Jamaica to re-enter the United States as a landed immigrant with a Green Card.

I visited my family in Nine Miles and Nesta in Trench Town. I visited my daughter Pearl, who was now nearly two years old and still under Enid's care, in Nine Miles. Everyone was joyful to see me looking so prosperous, married, and getting along so well in America. And I was glad to visit the old haunts of my childhood and see Puppa again as well as my sisters, brothers, and umpteen nieces and nephews who had come into the world since I had been away from Nine Miles in Kingston and Delaware.

Nesta was a Rasta, but he did not look ferocious and wicked. His hair was long, but it had not become a lion's mane of tangled braids. Although he was taken up deeply in his music, when I told him that Mr Booker would sponsor him too, he was quite keen on getting his papers even though he said he wasn't ready to leave Jamaica just yet. So we went to the government office to get him a passport and begin the long process of gaining him an entry visa to the US.

That day something happened that changed the name Nesta would be known by to the world. We had filled out the application for a passport and waited for hours to see a clerk who would complete the necessary paperwork. Finally, we inched our way forward in the line in the grubby government office and found ourselves sitting beside the desk of the fussy clerk, who was poring over the papers.

'Nesta?' the clerk suddenly snorted, reading the application. 'What kind o' name is dat?'

'How you mean what kind of name?' I asked. 'Is him natural name given him by his father.'

'You mean to tell me, Ma'am,' the clerk said scornfully, 'dat you want to carry dis young man to America under dat name?'

'What wrong with de name?'

'Is a girl name, is what wrong with it! You can't carry dis grown man to America under a girl name. Dem will laugh after him.'

Nesta shuffled his feet and said nothing.

'So what me should do, den?' I asked despairingly, for I knew that if you got on the wrong side of a clerk in a Jamaican government office, he could give you a warm time and humbug up your business.

'What him middle name?' the clerk asked, shuffling the papers as if he'd suddenly had an inspiration.

'Robert.'

'Now, see! Dere's a good name for a man. Bob! Solid like a rock – like de name of a man should be. None of dis Nesta, Lester, Chester foolishness. I going put down him name on de passport as Robert Nesta Marley.'

'If you think dat's better,' I mumbled lamely.

'I don't have to think. I *know* dat's better,' he announced confidently, completing the papers in a nice clerical hand with pretty curlicues and boasty squiggles.

Bam! bam! bam! he went with the official stamp on the papers and Nesta Robert Marley stood up and shuffled away to wait in the next line, his name having been changed by an unknown clerk to what the world would know him as to the end of his life – Bob Marley.

But Nesta wasn't ready to leave Jamaica quite yet. He thought he was on the verge of breaking out with his music. His prospects seemed plentiful and promising. So I left without him. But I had laid the groundwork to get him and Pearl to America with me. Shortly afterwards Pearl joined me, being brought in by a girl I knew named Jenny. And Nesta continued to struggle to make his name in Jamaican music.

'Whenever you ready,' I told him, 'just write and tell me, and I'll send you a ticket.'

Mr Booker and I had by now set up our household and were getting along lovingly as man and wife. Nesta and I continued to correspond. One evening, I came home to find in our mailbox a notice of attempted delivery of a registered letter. Mr Booker took me down to the post office to get it. The letter was from Nesta and contained a new US$10 bill.

In the letter Nesta tried to explain how singing his music made him feel: he said that when he sang he felt a spirit moving him just as it moved me in church, with the same joy and lightness in his soul. He wrote that the music business in Jamaica was still hard but said that lately he'd gotten a little money and he wanted to put some of it into my hands, even though he knew it wasn't much.

The whole way home I was crying over this letter. 'He's a good boy,' Mr Booker said comfortingly, patting me on the hands between driving. 'He's trying his best. He's a good boy.'

'You know how hard it is to get American money nowadays in Jamaica?' I wept.

Later, when Nesta became a big star, he would put thousands into my hands. He would buy me four houses, a shop in Delaware, spend thousands to give me the roof I now have over my head. But no amount of money he ever gave me – no matter how much – ever touched me as much as that lowly $10 bill.

Some months later Nesta wrote again to say that he'd met a nice girl named Rita and that she had become pregnant for him, and that if she had his baby he intended to marry her. I wrote him back and told him that he didn't have to marry any girl just because she had gotten pregnant for him, that marriage was a big step to be taken cautiously, and preferably only for love.

Soon afterwards, Rita began writing me long friendly letters and we started a regular correspondence. I heard later that she had lost the baby, which made me feel that I had given Nesta the right advice about not hastily marrying just because of some so-called pregnancy.

The months rolled past, and I began hearing rumors about Nesta from Jamaica. One day somebody – I believe it was my brother Gibson – came and told me that it was all over the news in Jamaica that Nesta had gotten married.

'Married?' I scoffed. 'And me don't know? Me no think so. If him get married, he no would tell him Mamma?'

And for a while, I heard nothing from Nesta about his plans to come to America or about any marriage. And whenever I wrote and asked if he wanted to come to America, I would hear back from him that he wasn't ready yet.

Meanwhile, the times continued brutally hard in Jamaica. Nesta's music had made a name for him on the island, but somebody else was pocketing all the money while he was ending up with small-change.

Then one day, he suddenly wrote and said he was ready to

come to America and try his luck. I quickly made the arrangements and mailed him an airplane ticket. A few months later Nesta joined me in Delaware.

Chapter Eleven

Nesta arrived in Philadelphia one winter night. I, Mr Booker, Jenny, who was still living with us at the time, and Enid from Jamaica – not my sister but the other Enid – went to pick him up at the airport. We were all overjoyed to see each other again, and one piece of hugging up and kissing up went on in the airport and spilled over into the parking lot. On the way home everyone was laughing and joking, talking about old times and catching up with the present. There was so much merriment in the long drive back to Wilmington it was like we were all drunk.

When we arrived home, everyone was eager to show Nesta around the house and ran from kitchen to drawing-room, babbling excitedly while he marveled at the layout and spaciousness of his new home, especially the bathrooms. Nesta followed Jenny and Enid around, exclaiming, 'Boy, de house nice, eh?'

When I caught up with them in the hallway, Nesta suddenly turned serious and said to me, 'Mamma, I vision dis house here, you know?'

'Oh yes?' I said. 'When you vision it?'

He walked around, staring at every hallway and into every room. He looked especially long and hard at the staircase before saying in a voice of wonderment, 'Same way I vision it last night! See dis staircase here! In me vision, I was walking it up two tread at a time.'

As if acting out his vision, he climbed the staircase two steps at a time, bounding to the top. I followed him up the stairs. The others remained below, drinking beer and celebrating.

'Same way me vision de place last night, Mamma! Same way!' Nesta continued to marvel like he could hardly believe his own powers.

He stopped at the doorway of a bedroom and asked, 'Whose room is dis?'

'Dis is your room,' I said.

'And who live over dere?' He pointed to another bedroom.

'Dat's Jenny and Pearl's room,' I said. 'And in de front room is me and Mr Booker.'

'Boy,' he whistled softly, 'de place nice!'

'See de bathroom over here,' I explained, going down the hall and showing him.

We stood in the doorway, peering in at the tiled bathroom with its porcelain tub and shower.

'Mamma,' Nesta said softly, standing right behind me, 'me married, you know?'

'You married?'

'Yes, through me was coming, me decide to marry. If you see de girl, you'll like her. She come from a nice family.'

'Well,' I said after a pause, 'is a pity you didn't tell me.'

He explained to me, in an embarrassed voice, that he'd gotten married at the urging of Coxson Dodd and in such haste that he really hadn't even had time to tell me. He said all this with a sheepish look as we stood in the hallway outside the upstairs bathroom.

'Well,' I said, 'if you married, you married. Now you here with us. So make us go celebrate downstairs.'

And we went downstairs to celebrate Nesta's marriage and his coming to America.

Nesta had come to America to earn money. He wanted to buy some instruments and music equipment to take back to Jamaica to help with his musical career. He had arrived in the dead of winter when there was a bite in the breeze and snow on the ground.

That first night Mr Booker and I huddled at the kitchen table and talked about what kind of work Nesta could get. We knew a Jamaican who worked as a stevedore on the waterfront, and I wondered if through that contact Nesta could get a job. Mr Booker said that stevedores were well paid, but he had his doubts about whether the boss would think Nesta strong enough to do the heavy lifting required, for all the dock-workers he'd ever known were big and muscular. We phoned our Jamaican contact and he said yes, Nesta could come down the next day, and if the boss liked his looks, he might get work.

The next morning I woke up with what I thought was a brilliant idea: to hide his slight build, I would pad up Nesta with bulky clothes. When I was done with him, he'd look as muscular as any old-time dock-worker.

I dressed him up in thick socks, three shirts, three pants, four sweaters, and gave him a pair of big canvas boots to wear, thinking they would add to his burly look. He was padded up so thickly that his arms stuck out like a robot; when he tried to walk in the oversized boots and three pants, he made a loud rustling noise and waddled like a muscle-bound weight-lifter. With nearly every step, he wobbled.

'Now you look like you have meat 'pon you bones.' I patted him on the back encouragingly. 'All you have to do is walk like Popeye, like you have plenty muscle.'

Full of hope and waddling like a penguin, Nesta stepped out into the wintry world of Delaware to be dropped off at the docks by Mr Booker, who was on his way to his own job at a car dealership.

Nesta was gone for some hours. The morning stretched into late afternoon. It got colder, and a wintry wind slashed through the bare, frozen streets like a razor blade.

I was getting dinner ready when I heard a sharp pounding at the front door. It was Nesta, standing on the doorstep, shivering and trembling from head to toe. His fingers were shriveled up; his face was raw-looking and had turned an ugly red.

'Nesta?' I cried, opening the door and letting him in. 'What happen? How you reach home?'

Between his violent shivering and clattering teeth, he stuttered the story: the boss had said he wasn't dressed properly for working on the waterfront. He was wearing the wrong kind of boots, which could cause him to slip and fall into the cargo hole of a ship and get hurt. Plus, the boss had seen through the piles of padding and judged him too slightly built for the kind of heavy lifting involved in dock work.

'So, how you reach home?' I cried, rushing him to the radiator and rubbing his back and shoulders to help him get warm.

He said that he had returned on foot, that he had passed a gang of hooligan boys on a street corner who had looked like they were out for trouble, and when he saw them staring at him, he had run all the way home.

My heart was racing. I couldn't believe that he'd been able to find his way back all by himself, for this was the first morning he had ever left the house. I didn't know how to get him warm. He was shivering uncontrollably under the ridiculous bulky clothes like he was having an attack of fits.

'Lawd Jesus!' I bawled. 'Wha' me fe do now?'

I quickly rang up Mr Booker at work and explained what had happened.

'Him finger look like dem going drop off!' I wailed.

'There's only one thing for that,' Mr Booker said. 'Take him outside and make him push his frozen hands in the snow.'

'Say what?'

'That's the cure for frostbite, Ciddy,' Mr Booker said calmly. 'Nesta has frostbite. He needs to push his hands in the snow. That will dry them out. Keep them away from heat.'

'Push him hand inna de snow! Put punkas 'pon pankas? Him hand cold enough already!'

'Put what on what?' Mr Booker asked, puzzled. He always used to complain that he couldn't understand me when I got excited and started talking Jamaican. What I meant was that Nesta's frozen hands would get only colder if he put them in a snowdrift. I would be adding trouble (punkas) to the same kind of trouble (pankas).

I hurriedly made Nesta some hot tea and gave him to drink. And eventually, after thawing by the radiator, he was able to flex his fingers, and the color returned to his face as the raw redness gradually drained from his complexion.

That was the end of Nesta's attempt to become a dock-worker. He obviously needed an inside job, especially during these brutal winter months, for his Jamaican blood just couldn't cope with the icebox called Delaware.

We had to try something else.

Eventually, after some trying, Nesta got a job as a janitor at the Dupont Hotel and settled down to work his daily shift and save his money. When he was off from work, he would sit quietly in the drawing-room or the kitchen, strumming his guitar and writing songs. Sometimes he would ask me to harmonize a song with him, and the two of us would sing it together. He would pause over a line and ask me what I thought or if I had a better way of putting that particular feeling. Yet even though he was always strumming his guitar and singing, he was still as quiet as a church mouse, and if it wasn't for the sound of the guitar, nobody would even know he was at home.

One day Mr Booker suddenly said to me that he thought Nesta didn't like him.

'Why you say dat?' I asked, alarmed.

'Because,' Mr Booker complained, 'whenever I walk into a room where he's playing, he immediately gets up and leaves.

It's like he doesn't want to be in the same room with me.'

I told Nesta what Mr Booker had said. Nesta explained that he thought his constant strumming as he searched for new licks and riffs on the guitar would annoy Mr Booker. The truth was, I told him, just the opposite: Mr Booker found the sound of the guitar very restful on his nerves after a hard day at work. When he found that out, Nesta would no longer leave the room where he was practicing if Mr Booker entered it, but continue this strumming, even though he would occasionally look self-conscious as he worked to compose a new song.

As the years passed, Mr Booker and Nesta grew to be good friends. In fact, many times later on when Nesta was visiting, Mr Booker would point to Richard and Anthony, our two young sons playing on the floor, and say to Nesta, 'If anything happens to me, take care of my boys.'

And a few years later when Mr Booker died, Nesta, up to the moment of his own untimely passing, faithfully honored Mr Booker's request.

By the time Nesta arrived to live with me in Delaware, he was a practicing Rasta, but not an impractical one. He had his beliefs, but he held them quietly and did not try to push them off on me or anyone else. For example, before he went job hunting, I suggested to him that he needed to get his hair trimmed, and he put up no argument or fuss. I took him to the barber, who trimmed his locks ear-length. Immediately afterwards, Nesta got the janitorial job at Dupont.

Yet on some teachings of his Rasta religion, Nesta was firm. One morning as I was frying up some bacon, Nesta came into the kitchen, glanced at the stove and said quietly, 'Is a dangerous something dat, you know, Mamma.'

'Dangerous? How bacon dangerous?'

'It come from de swine where Jesus cast de devil. Is a unclean animal.'

'It taste good, though,' I joked.

'No, Mamma!' he said firmly. 'No fry nothing inna dat pot for me to eat, 'cause me nah eat it.' Indeed, Nesta was so against pork eating that he wouldn't eat any foods that were even cooked in a pot that had been used earlier to cook pork.

Yet he had said this in a mild, not a quarrelsome, voice, and I couldn't argue with his beliefs, seeing as how he felt them so strongly, for even in those days, Nesta was trying his best to stick with Ital cooking, which is a natural way of cooking practiced by Rastas. Nevertheless, he was not hard to please, and the only meal where he might have been a little picky-picky was breakfast, for he could not eat eggs, since they were against him, and he would not eat bacon because it came from the pig. But he loved a cornmeal or banana porridge. Or he would eat toast and jam and fruit and drink juice.

At other moments during Nesta's stay with me in Delaware, we discussed religion. I was, and had been from girlhood days, a faithful follower of the Pentecostal Church. Mr Booker was a staunch Baptist. He went to his church, and I to mine. Everyone knew that I loved my Sabbath services and that occasionally the spirit would seize ahold of me and make me speak loudly in tongues. When it came to religion, Nesta knew me as a prayerful woman with a mighty love of God.

One day as we were reasoning in the drawing-room, Nesta said, 'You know, Mamma, is hard for me to tell you dat Haile Selassie is God. Because you come up from a little child and hear everybody worship Jesus, Jesus, and me is your son and you claim you older dan me and you know more dan me. But from de day you born, Mamma, you is a Rasta, and as time goes on, you'll get the realization that Haile Selassie is God.'

'Nesta,' I replied, 'I think His Majesty is a great man. But I don't think he's God.'

'So who is God?' he asked quietly.

'Who is God?'

'Yes. Who is God? You ever see God?'

'No,' I admitted, 'but I feel God spiritually, though I never lay me own eye upon him.'

'So how you know His Majesty Haile Selassie I is not God?'

I was stumped: it was just a simple question, but I had no answer.

'Mamma,' he said with conviction, 'God is black. His Majesty Haile Selassie I is earth rightful ruler. All dese years, dem tell you lie 'bout God. God is black.'

It was a hard message for me to accept – at first.

But this was the way Jah had planned it. He had sent my son down to earth as a messenger to teach the path of enlightenment and truth, to strip the veil of falsehood and darkness from the eye of the unbeliever. Soon Nesta's teachings would lift the burdens from my shoulders and show me the way of righteousness. And even when I stood blocking the door, Nesta would gently remove me and reveal unto me the right road to the kingdom. As it is written, 'What is hidden from the wise and prudent is revealed to the babe and suckling.' Nesta was, at that moment of private reasoning with me in the drawing-room, about his Father's business.

I didn't grasp the truth of Nesta's message then. It was only later that I would see the truth with the new-found eyes of the trusting babe. For now, my mind was still captured by the image of Jesus – the white God with the bleeding heart punctured by a wreath of thorns – whose picture had hung over my bed-head throughout the long years of my childhood. That was what God looked like to me: it was Nesta who would teach me that the Godhead once manifested in Jesus had come again to walk the earth in the human form of His Majesty Haile Selassie. It was only later that I would grasp that my first-born son was also my father and teacher and the revealer unto me of Jah's truth.

During those early days before I grasped the truth of Nesta's message, I would inveigle him to come with me to church.

Sometimes he would say with a smile, 'Me no go to dem kind o' church, you know.'

'Come wid me, still,' I urged, 'for today is Sunday and you nah do nothing.'

Sometimes he would just shrug and accompany me to service.

He liked some things about my church. For example, he liked that we knelt down and prayed quietly in the pews before taking our seats. But usually he would whisper to me during the service, 'You see all dem boy up dere inna de pulpit say dem a preach, you think anyone o' dem could baptize me? Dem is little boy looking money, you no see dat?'

And even though I would mutter to him that it was disrespectful to call the minister a 'little boy', I would also remember that many years earlier, Captain, Nesta's father, had spoken nearly the same words about the parson of the Shiloh church. And in my deepest heart I would marvel but hold my peace.

Years later, I would also see Captain again in one of Nesta's songs. Nesta had a hit song, 'Talking Blues', in which he wrote these lines:

> *Cold ground was my bed last night,*
> *and rock stone was my pillow, too.*

When I first heard that song, I thought immediately of something his father often said during his frequent weepy moods. He would say,

> *Stones for my pillow,*
> *and the sky is my roof.*

and cry like his heart would break. He often repeated those lines when the mood of sadness was upon him, and they never failed to bring water pouring from his eyes.

A woman once told me that Nesta had written those lines after being thrown in jail by the police, but he denied that. When

I asked him if he'd ever been locked up by the police in Jamaica, he told me that he would have been many times, except that he would always humble himself before the officers and they would let him go.

I myself believed him. I don't think he wrote those lyrics from experience. I think it was his father's spirit emerging through Nesta's song. But I also think that Nesta, like the rest of us, had two fathers – Captain, who implanted the seed in my womb that became our son, and Jah, who sent Nesta down to earth as his messenger to spread and teach His truth. And in the songs he left behind for the world to hear and heed were mingled the earthly spirit of his father, who was of the flesh, and the heavenly spirit of Jah, who is not of this kingdom, but who is the maker and caretaker of all that moves and breathes upon the earth.

On this visit, too, Nesta had a vision in which his two fathers, of earth and of heaven, were mixed and which I at first found confusing. It happened when he was waiting to hear from Dupont about the application he had made for employment.

One evening I came home from work at about 3.30 p.m. and found Nesta watching television in the drawing-room. I invited him to come with me to the grocery store, but he said no, he would stay in case Dupont called.

I left and went to do my shopping. When I returned, he met me at the door.

'Mamma,' he said, as he helped me unload groceries in the kitchen, 'you know, since you gone, me lie down here, and me have a vision.'

'Oh yes?' I remarked. 'What you vision?'

He said a short man wearing a khaki cloak and a mash-up mash-up hat had appeared to him in his vision. Walking over to where Nesta lay dozing on the couch, the man had put his hand in his pocket and taken out a ring. Then, leaning over, and without saying a word, the man had carefully placed the ring on Nesta's finger.

I said, 'You vision dat since me gone?'

He nodded.

'You know who dat man is?' I asked.

He shook his head.

'Is you Daddy,' I explained. 'Him put dat ring 'pon you finger because him give you nothing in life. Him never have nothing to give. But him come now to give you him blessing.'

Nesta glanced at a ring I had on my finger – it was a black ring – and remarked that the ring the man had placed on his finger had looked like my onyx ring, black same way, but nicer and richer-looking. And he was feeling good about his vision and my explanation of the blessing he had been given by his father. For myself, I was delighted that he'd gotten such a vision, which showed that his father continued to take an interest in our son's welfare.

But my interpretation was wrong, and the fullness of time would soon prove the true identity of the man in Nesta's vision when many years afterwards Nesta was given a ring by the grandson of His Majesty Haile Selassie I; it was a black ring with a gold lion embedded in its center, and it had once been worn on the finger of His Majesty. Nesta reported to me that sometimes the ring burned his finger like it was on fire. And once when we were discussing old times, Nesta asked me if I recalled the vision he'd had in Delaware where a man appeared unto him who I thought was his father.

I said yes, I remembered it well.

'Dat wasn't me father, Mamma,' he said painfully, for his sickness was by then heavy upon him and wearing down his earthly body. 'Dat was His Majesty Haile Selassie I.'

Nesta guarded this dream ring closely. When it had to come off his finger during the days of his sickness and treatment, he entrusted it to his lawyer and friend, Diane Jobson, whom he always trusted with the dearest treasures of his life, and begged her to watch it carefully for him.

When Nesta died, there was some squabble among the heirs over this valuable ring. Some insistent voices clamored that it belonged among the assets of the estate. But Diane stepped in and declared that the ring belonged only one place: on the finger where His Majesty, through his grandson and in a vision, had placed it.

The ring was buried with Nesta and lies today with his mortal remains in his tomb at Nine Miles in the mountains of Jamaica.

Nesta stayed with me in Delaware for nine months. He went to work every day, practiced his music constantly, and saved his money. Aside from the company of the immediate family, he kept mainly to himself. Sometimes on his day off he would sit quietly and read the Bible, for Rastas are known for their biblical study and reasoning, and to back up his opinions on doctrine, he was able to quote chapter and verse of scripture.

The months flew past; Rita wrote him often, and he would answer her back in a short note, for Nesta was not one to write long letters. Soon he became a little restless and moody, and it was obvious to me that he was beginning to miss Jamaica, Rita, and the music scene. One day he said it was time for him to go home. I didn't argue with him or try to talk him into extending his stay. Nesta was now a big man with his own life. He knew where he was supposed to be, and anyone could see that he belonged in only one place – in Jamaica.

The months dwindled into weeks, the weeks into days, and then the appointed hour of his return had come. Mr Booker and I drove him back to the airport in Philadelphia, and this time the journey was quiet, with no happy chatter to fill it. In the trunk of the car was the valuable musical equipment he had swept the floors of the Dupont Hotel to buy.

At the airport, we hugged and said goodbye. My eye-water

flowed, but I did my best to hide it. I was pregnant with Richard, who would become Mr Booker's first-born, and I didn't want to disturb the infant with my sadness. Then Nesta boarded the plane and was gone again out of my life.

Mr Booker and I drove slowly back to Wilmington. Once again winter was upon the land. The world was gray and dim, and a light snow dusted the windscreen of the car on the long and lonely drive back home.

Chapter Twelve

Nesta's life-story is closely tied up with his marriage to Rita Marley. Once, they were young lovers who sang and toured together. Once, they suffered want together as they struggled for the material goods of life. They sang songs and had children, Rita bearing a daughter, Cedella, and two sons, Ziggy and Steve, for Nesta. They were shot together in the assassination attempt of 1976. As I look back at their life, they seem to me to have been happier during the early years of hardship than they were during the later years of riches and fame.

In the end, their days would be marked by bitterness and strife. But I can say, without a doubt, that of all the women in Nesta's life, his strongest and most abiding love, down to the last breath he drew on this earth, was for Rita Marley.

Nesta was now a grown man, with a wife and his own family. Rita bore him a daughter, his first-born child, and the infant was called Cedella after me. Shortly after Nesta left Delaware, I myself had a son for Mr Booker, and we christened our child Richard.

During those days, Nesta and I kept in touch through Rita's letter-writing, which fed me a constant diet of news about the family in Jamaica. Even though Nesta was gradually making a name for himself throughout the Caribbean as a songwriter and performer, I gathered that his music was still nothing more than a hand-to-mouth existence. In fact, it was only after Nesta had signed with Chris Blackwell and Island Records that he would become an international star.

However, things between Nesta and Rita were not running smoothly. Open war had not yet broken out, but serious and regular battling was raging. I caught background rumbles in Rita's letters in which she would complain about Nesta's neglectfulness and the many hours he spent away reasoning with the brethren day and night when she felt he should have been at home with his wife and daughter. Sometimes she would write bitterly about a particular incident; often she would complain about always being left alone.

There is an old Jamaican saying, 'Puss don't business in dog fight,' meaning that some situations you don't belong in and should stay out of. Nesta was my son, but he was also a grown man who had to manage his woman in his own way. Plus with me being in Delaware and Nesta being in Jamaica, there wasn't much I could do to settle his differences with Rita.

But things between them went from bad to worse and soon Rita wrote and asked if I could come to Jamaica and try to restore peace. Rita said it was Nesta's idea. Later, Nesta would claim that the idea was Rita's. However, both said that they thought it would be nice if I saw my namesake granddaughter, Cedella.

I said yes, I would come. And a few weeks later I went.

I landed in Kingston late at night, weary from traveling with two small children – Pearl, who was then only a few years old, and my newborn son, Richard.

Nesta and Rita met me at the airport, and I laid eyes on Nesta's wife for the first time face to face. At the airport terminal she ran up to hug and greet me, saying sweetly, 'Hi, Mom!' and I felt like I'd met her somewhere, sometime before. Standing before me was a slim, pretty, young girl whose smile showed beautiful teeth and whose hair was tied up under a tam. Since that first meeting, 'Mom' is what Rita has always called me.

Nesta was a little standoffish because he was so well known throughout Jamaica that wherever he went people would be gawking at him, and he was always conscious and shy about being stared at in public. But he gave me a hug too, and we bundled into his car and had a warm reunion in private.

I stayed with my Aunt Ivy on Hagley Park Road because Nesta was still struggling, and the little house he occupied with Rita couldn't hold me and two small children. The next evening, Nesta and Rita visited, bringing dinner for us as well as medicine for Richard, who was down with a cold and fever.

Later that night, the four of us – Nesta, the son I had borne for Captain, Pearl, the daughter I'd had for Mr Taddy, and Richard, the first-born son I'd given Mr Booker, and I – found ourselves alone for a few moments in a small back bedroom while Rita and Aunt Ivy took an airing on the verandah. Nesta lay down on a couch and looked over at the bed where I sat comforting Richard, who was fussy-fussy from being sick.

'You know what, Mamma?' Nesta said softly.

'What?'

'Is so all of we should live together all de time.'

'Dat would be nice,' I murmured, touched.

In the night we could hear the background rumble of traffic from Hagley Park Road over the heartbeat of a distant sound system. For a brief while, all of us in that room were suspended in a quiet moment of warm family feeling.

But as quickly as the moment came, it went. Rita entered into the room to see what we were doing, and the warm feeling fluttered out the window like a night-time moth returning to its nest of darkness.

That visit to Jamaica was the first time I saw for myself the run-ins between Rita and Nesta. From this visit, it was obvious to me that the relationship between them was under pressure.

Over the passing years, it would have its ups and downs, getting worse rather than better.

All of the many reasons why their life together never ran smoothly, some of which came out on that first visit, basically boiled down to one point: Nesta never wanted to be married. The idea that he was a married man stuck in his craw, especially since Nesta felt that he had been forced into marriage by Coxson Dodd and trickery.

I saw this then; I would hear it out of his own mouth later, sometimes with venom. One time, for example, when Nesta was visiting me in Delaware, he came into my drawing-room and saw some wedding pictures of him and Rita on display in a frame on the mantelpiece.

'Hey!' he said gruffly. 'No put dem thing up here fe man to see.' He took down the frame, opened it up, removed the wedding pictures, tore them into pieces and threw them in the trash.

'Why you do dat?' I asked him. 'Is you married picture!'

He kissed his teeth with contempt. 'Married?' he said scornfully. 'Married what?'

I didn't understand this attitude at first, certainly not on this visit. Later I found out what Nesta was thinking and why he felt resentment over being married.

One day, years later, Nesta and I were talking about his relationship with Rita and their up-and-down marriage. Nesta suddenly looked suspicious and confused.

'Mamma,' he blurted out, 'I don't even know how it happen, dat me married.'

'How could you not know how it happen?'

The whole story came pouring out of him.

He said that the day he supposedly got married, an old woman from the district of Greenwich Farm suddenly came up to him in the yard, took his hand, and kissed the back of it. Later he found out that the woman was a Madda – an obeah woman who practices Jamaican voodoo. He said that after the Madda had kissed his hand, something strange happened, for the next thing he knew, people were telling him that he was married to Rita Marley.

After Nesta had told me the story, I said to him, 'Nesta, listen to me. If dis marriage between you and Rita is something dem do to make happen, it not going work out, it going to sunder. For what is not planted by God's hand going surely root up.'

However, it would only be years later that I'd understand fully how Nesta felt about his marriage. At that time, I didn't know about the Madda, and therefore his bitter remarks about supposedly being married made no sense.

On this trip, for example, I witnessed an argument between Nesta and Rita in which he made a scornful remark that I didn't understand then but would become clear later when he told me about the Madda. I don't know what sparked that particular argument, but I remember hearing Nesta scoff contemptuously as he stood in the doorway glaring at Rita. 'Married? You think me could married and me modder don't know?'

I interrupted. 'Well,' I said, 'whether me know or me don't know, de two o' you married and it done. No bodder quarrel over dis.'

It was one of many fusses that I witnessed between them and tried my best to sort out, usually with only temporary success. Sometimes Rita would cry and run out of the room. Nesta would glower and look furious. But usually when I came to where I heard them raging with one another, the argument would sputter to a stop, leaving both of them seething.

Rita's complaints that she made to me on this visit were typical of the ones you hear from young married people. She said that Nesta neglected her to gallivant around town. She claimed that sometimes she didn't see him for two or three days, that he would leave her alone in a rented house to take care of the baby by herself.

Another source of vexation to Rita were Nesta's close ties to his Rasta brethren and their practices. She bitterly told me that Nesta had taken Cedella to a Rasta priest to be baptized, and the man had blown herb smoke (ganja or marijuana) in the baby's face as part of the ceremony.

Nesta had his side, too. His defense was that he was only looking after his music and couldn't be two places at once, that Rita didn't understand that he had work to do. But even when he was away, Nesta said, his family was always on his mind and in his thoughts. To prove that this was true, he told me a story.

He said one day he had been in Coxson's studio, recording for hours. Darkness fell and he suddenly felt tired. Since it was nightfall, he lay down on a cot in the studio to catch a rest. But no sooner had he closed his eyes, Nesta said, than he visioned a scorpion crawling towards the bed on which Sharon, Rita's young daughter with an earlier lover, slept.

He said he jumped up out from the cot and said aloud to himself, 'But wait! Wha' kind a dream me dream?'

The vision upset him so much that he rushed immediately to the house he was then renting in Trench Town and went into Sharon's room, where she lay sound asleep. Turning on the light, he searched the room and found a scorpion on the wall, inching towards the baby. He quickly picked up the sleeping child and carried her into another room. Then he returned to her bedroom and killed the scorpion.

Behind all of Rita's complaints I also sensed a jealousy over other women, and during this trip that feeling also came out. Nesta's answer, as he told me later in one of my private chats with him as I tried to patch up their differences, was a simple one: 'You see, me, Mamma?' he said. 'Me out dere up and down wid de people when me do me music. And thousands and thousands of women love me. But me can't stop people from loving me. And is not every woman me could love, either.'

He added, 'If me goin' have a woman 'round me as me woman and she goin' act like a Jezebel, den she always goin' have something to worry and fuss about.'

And so the fussing went, from one side to the other. Sometimes I would hear voices raised in anger in another room. But as soon as they heard or saw me coming to see what this latest row was all about, they would immediately stop their quarreling even though Rita would continue to sob and Nesta would look cross.

Rita had been raised by a strict woman named Auntie Viola, who was also then living under their roof. Between Nesta and Auntie always ran mistrust and tension. Nesta feared Auntie because he thought she was a Madda. Auntie also feared Nesta.

When I first met her, Auntie took me aside and immediately began complaining about what she said was Nesta's quarrelsome and outrageous behavior. She was just beginning to get down to cases when we heard footsteps coming down the walkway. Glancing out the window, Auntie caught a glimpse of Nesta approaching. Her hand flew to her mouth. With a gasp, she darted out the back door and disappeared.

On this trip I also met some of Nesta's musical friends. I met Peter Tosh and renewed acquaintances with Bunny Wailer. One evening there was a knock at the gate and both of them were there, waiting to see Nesta, who called me out of the house to meet them. I stood and chatted with them for a few minutes, exchanging pleasantries with Bunny, whom I had not seen for a long while. That evening, Peter was on his best bahavior. Later he would develop a wicked mouth for bad words and blasphemy.

After we had chatted at the gate for a while, I returned to the house. Behind me I heard Peter say to Nesta, 'Hmm! She look all right.' I took the remark as a compliment.

I stayed with Nesta for about two weeks on that visit and witnessed what was going on between him and Rita. I tried to give what advice I could and often told them, 'Stop de fussing and live in peace with one anodder.' They would listen and nod and everything would quiet down for a while. Then the fire would catch up again and start to blaze over some little act, word, or gesture. So it would go on and off throughout their whole life. So it continued to go when I finally left them and returned to Delaware and Mr Booker, taking with me my two children, Pearl and Richard.

Nesta and Rita drove me to the airport. In the terminal before boarding my plane, I gave them a final dose of the only medicine I had to give. 'Try to understand one anodder and not fuss so much. See one side and de odder. Look 'pon de odder point of view.'

They nodded respectfully as if I were saying wise words. But nothing between them would ever be changed by words out of any mouth.

In affairs of the heart, even a mother becomes a bystander.

About two years later Nesta and Rita joined me in Delaware, bringing with them Cedella and Ziggy, who was then still a baby. Rita was pregnant with Steve, but not yet showing.

They'd had a long and wearying flight with many stop-overs, and when we met them at the airport, both Nesta and Rita were frazzled and fussy-fussy. Nesta complained that Rita had embarrassed him by breast-feeding Ziggy on the plane, causing a man strolling down the aisle to turn and stare. Rita snapped that the baby was hungry, and what was she to do, she was a breast-feeding mother.

We quieted them down and drove quickly to Wilmington, where everyone turned in early with jangled nerves and enjoyed a good night's sleep. The next morning, we all awoke in a better mood and had a real reunion.

Our house was now lively with the noise of five small romping children. There were Cedella and Ziggy – Nesta and Rita's children – Sharon, Rita's child with another man, and Pearl and Richard, my daughter with Mr Taddy and my son with Mr Booker.

Rita and Nesta had come to get ahead and soon both of them went job-hunting. Rita landed a job as a housekeeper, and Nesta one in the Chrysler factory, putting in screws in cars on the assembly line.

By this time, Rita and Nesta were full-fledged Rastas. In fact, Auntie had already warned me in a letter that Rita never allowed comb to touch her hair and went about the streets looking like a teggereg (ruffian). Nesta's hair had grown long and was draping down in dreadlocks, giving him a handsome, manly look. Later, his full set of locks would become a sight to behold, and when he performed it would become his trademark to fling them wildly around on the stage as the spirit swept him up in song.

Before going to Chrysler to apply for a job, Nesta asked me to trim his locks so he would look presentable, and I did, carefully gathering the clippings into a paper bag for burial. Rastas always dispose of their locks this way, never simply discarding them in the trash. In fact, in some parts of Jamaica, people believe that if you throw away your hair clippings, birds will gather them to build their nests, turning you mad or into a bird-brain. I myself don't believe this but still I respect those Rastas who prefer to bury their locks when it is necessary to cut them.

During their stay with us, poor Mr Booker was often confused by the sound of Jamaicans babbling in patois all throughout the house, and would often look baffled and ask, 'What? What?' repeatedly.

Peace had still not come to Nesta and Rita. Sometimes they would fuss and I'd hear Rita wailing upstairs and go to see what was the matter, but always they would quiet down when they heard my footsteps because they knew that my blood pressure had gotten so high that I'd lost my job as a nurse's aide in an old people's home.

In all of these arguments I'd feel sorry for Rita, for she would always bawl that she had no mother, and I would try and comfort her as a mother would. Yet in most of their fusses, they wouldn't share the full grievance with me, for fear of upsetting me further. I'd always tell them not to hold anything back from me, for if I didn't know now, I'd know later. Plus if they shared the trouble with me, I could start working on it in prayer, and when I set my heart to it and kneel to pray, wonders happen.

Rita's housekeeping job sometimes required her to stay overnight, and one day we bundled in the car and went to look for her. She was working as a maid for an elderly, rich, white woman, who peeped through the window at the car full of black people parked before her house and got so frightened that she fired Rita. Fortunately, Rita got a job as a nurse's aide at a hospital, but she soon lost it because management objected to the way she wrapped her hair as a Rasta.

I had my little differences with Rita, but they were no more than mosquito bites. She got into the habit, for example, of spending a lot of time on Market Street, in a little African art shop located in an arty section of Wilmington, and she'd often leave me alone to take care of five small children who, when they were ready, could put up quite a squawk.

One day all five of them started crying at once, and Rita was nowhere to be found. I sent someone down to Market Street to bring her home, and when she returned I lit into her for leaving me alone with all five babies.

'Dem is fe you children, too, you know, Ma'am,' she sniped.

'Yes,' I snapped. 'But look! Me hand full! And meantime you down at Market Street giving laugh fe pea soup.'

That spat soon blew over, for I never felt any grudge against Rita, and to this day I don't hold any. Yet on this visit they were only marking time: in the back of my head, I knew that.

Nesta's true mission in this world was his music, and in every spare minute he practiced and composed. In fact, it was Nesta's music that caused the most serious rift between me and Rita, and to this day, if she has any grievance against me (and I hope she doesn't), it is over a remark I made during one of our many drawing-room rehearsals.

Nesta was rehearsing a new song, 'Splish for a Splash', and he asked me and Rita to harmonize it with him. But he still wasn't satisfied with the sound. When it came to his songs, he was a perfectionist. Repeatedly he kept asking Rita to sing a certain note. He grew more and more impatient with her as she struggled to hit the note.

'If you goin' sing de thing, sing it, nuh!' he growled.

'Bob, me can't sing it 'cause me no have de strength. Me weak,' Rita complained.

'Rita,' I said innocently, meaning nothing, 'me never know you can't sing.'

To this day, Rita sometimes still talks about that remark, which I had made with no malice or wicked thoughts, but innocently.

It was during this visit, too, that Nesta made friends with some local boys while playing football in the park for exercise, which, next to his music, was his other passion. They later told me that one day as they were catching their breath after a rugged football session, Nesta prophesied in an idle moment of chat that he expected to be dead by the age of thirty-six. Later, after Nesta had died at thirty-six, they remembered and told me about his grim prophecy.

The days flew past. Nesta got the call from Island Records to come to England and cut an album. Rita grew heavy with child. Soon Nesta was gone, and there was only Rita and their three children left with me at home.

Shortly after Nesta left for England, Rita gave birth to Steve.

Within a couple of weeks of Steve's arrival, two other children fathered by Nesta were also born in Jamaica. Robbie was born to Pat; Rohan, whom I would eventually adopt, was born to

Janet. Rita fretted that Nesta, who had planned to go to Jamaica before returning to Delaware, would know his other newborn sons before knowing her own. She was bitter about this, and nothing I said made her feel consoled.

Soon after Steve's birth, Rita returned to Jamaica. We had run into difficulties with her visa because it had been discovered that she was not born in Cuba, as we'd thought, making her eligible for refugee status, but in Jamaica. Moreover, Nesta was also in visa trouble, the immigration department having ruled that because he was now married and an adult, I couldn't sponsor him as a minor child.

So the family returned to Jamaica with things just as shaky as ever between Nesta and Rita.

The next time I saw them the sundering I expected had begun. But no one had told me anything. I found out because on my arrival at the airport, no one met me. I stood under the overhang of the terminal roof in Kingston while a wicked rain poured down without mercy, awaiting a ride that never came. Eventually, I took a taxi to their Bull Bay house.

Soon Nesta came to the house and began quarreling that no one had met me at the airport. That's when I realized: they're not living together. Rita was living in Bull Bay; Nesta, at 56 Hope Road.

There was also a new child, a little girl named Stephanie, born while Nesta was away in England on business, and one look at her told me that she wasn't his. Her father turned out to be a friend of Nesta's, a man named Tacky whom everyone called Ital.

In fact, on this visit I met the father, who drove a truck for a living and owned a house deep in the bush, and when I remarked to him one evening that he looked weary, he shrugged and said he was doing his best to support his daughter. Then he pointed to little Stephanie, innocently playing on the floor.

I could do nothing but gape. Yet I found Ital to be a very polite gentleman who always greeted me with respect, saying, 'How you do, Modder?' and one day, when he thought I might be short of funds, he gave me money to tide me over.

Nesta must have known that Stephanie was not his child. But Rita refused to admit it and continued in this stubbornness for years. Nesta fretted and fretted as though his heart would break. He kept pressing Rita: How could he be Stephanie's father? He had been in England. Who was the real father? Who? Inside, it ate away at him. He was like a man tormented by a truth too terrible to face.

One time, for example, Nesta called me from Germany where, now a successful and acclaimed performer with a worldwide following, he was on tour. His voice was tired and in pain. 'Mamma,' he said, 'I want a blood test of de baby.'

'Hear me now, Nesta,' I replied. 'Suppose you get a blood test and it show de baby not yours. Wa' you going do?'

'Get a divorce.'

The wires hummed between us across the ocean, but his voice quivered with pain I felt as sharply as if he stood at my side.

'Nesta,' I counseled, 'you see de whole o' you 'pon tour. And I don't think you should be worrying you brain 'bout dis now when you out dere touring. Just see if you can hold youself together and do what you have to do and no get involve in all dis kind o' mix-up mix-up. Don't bring down no pressure 'pon youself.'

Nor did Rita even try to hide her relationship with Ital. One time, for example, she came to me and boasted about a ring that Ital had given her, and she flashed it off to me on her finger. I never mentioned this episode to Nesta, for Jah has given me the overstanding (not *understanding*, for one who grasps truth is not *under* but *over* it) to deal with people, and I would have only been spreading jealousy and strife.

Yet part of the torment Nesta felt over Rita's unfaithfulness was due to his nature as a man. Once another man had entered a woman of his, Nesta would drop her for ever. That was the way he was with Pat, Robbie's mother; that was how he was with Rita. But he just couldn't bring himself to believe that Rita, on paper still his wife, had taken a lover. And for years this unspoken truth tormented him.

One time, for example, when Rita and Nesta had their own house in Delaware beside mine, Nesta barged into my kitchen and wanted me to follow him next door to confront Rita about what Ital had said about having to support his daughter, Stephanie. It took all my overstanding of the human heart not to make matters between them worse that day.

Finally, one day Rita admitted to Nesta that Ital was the father of Stephanie. The admission was made while Nesta was on tour in California with the I-Threes – Judy Mowatt, Marcia Griffiths and Rita. After the truth came out, Nesta said to me ruefully, 'Imagine, it take Rita three years to tell me de truth. Three years!'

The anguish and hurt he felt over Rita pierced his heart like a dagger. I heard him singing a song once about being hurt, and I knew immediately what the words meant.

Rita had broken his heart.

The depths of Nesta's sadness over Rita showed during the final days of his sickness.

One day, a Friday, when we were in Germany at a rented house, Nesta and I had a quiet chat about his life. Sick with brain cancer and given up for dead by his American doctors, he was to be operated on the next day at the Issels clinic. Rita was also in Germany but had gone away to some city to promote her album, *One Draw*. Nesta was missing her.

We talked about their life together. Nesta complained that Rita had never washed a shirt for him, never cooked him a dinner, never boiled him a cup of tea. I asked him where he usually ate supper, and he replied here and there. I reminded him of the Jamaican proverb, 'Dog with too much owner go to bed without supper' (because each owner thinks the other will feed him). He chuckled and looked downhearted.

Finally, he stirred. 'Mamma,' he remarked bitterly, 'you no see it no make no sense dat Rita come here. For she nah do nothing fe me.'

I tried my best to cheer him up by saying, 'Nesta, she soon come back. But she say now dat you sick, she have fe earn de bread and butter.'

'Bread and butter,' he spat scornfully. 'She just come and she gone.'

He was quiet for a long while. Then he sighed and said mournfully, 'Boy! Rita! Hmm! When me meet Rita, Rita live inna one little shack inna Trench Town, full o' cockroach and rat. Me take her from dere, and me go buy place in Bull Bay give her. Me buy her property in Clarendon. Me buy her house on Washington Drive. Now she gone up on top of de hill.'

He fell into another brooding silence. Finally, he sighed and said softly, 'Mamma. Is Rita give me cancer.'

I was shocked. 'Nesta, what you saying to me? How could Rita give you cancer?'

'Imagine,' he continued, 'me left Rita and gone go work in England fe her, and when me gone Rita breed fe me friend.'

'Nesta,' I said, 'me never know dat you take it so hard.' I began to cry. I couldn't help myself, I was so torn up by all his terrible suffering. 'Rita got to pay you back,' I sobbed, 'for everything dat she do to you.'

'Pay me back? How she goin' pay me back?'

I was weeping helplessly. I searched for the right words. 'I don't know. Even if she have to wash you clothes and drink de water, she goin' have fe pay.'

When Rita returned from her promotion tour, I took her aside and told her what Nesta had said, that she had given him cancer.

Rita denied it. She said that Father (Jah) had given Nesta cancer because of his wickedness to her. She gave me one for-instance: she related how one time Seeco Patterson, one of the Wailers, told Nesta something she'd supposedly done. Enraged, Nesta bundled her into a car, and he and Seeco drove her at night to Palisadoes – the claw of land that encircles Kingston harbor. They walked her down to the windward side of the claw where the big waves crash daylight and darkness, scraping the shingle with wind, foam, and thunder. There, on that desolate stretch of ocean, Nesta ordered her to take her wedding ring off her finger and give it him. Then he flung it into the raging water while she wept and trembled on the beach.

Rita had just finished this tale when Nesta shuffled into the room looking sad and tired. 'We ready fe go now,' he muttered. And we drove him to the hospital where early the next morning he would undergo surgery.

That Saturday, Rita drove to Munich to buy flowers for Nesta: and she bought another two bunches, a big one for her, a small one for me. She also bought a plastic heart, for this was February and Valentine's Day was coming. She placed the plastic heart among the big bunch of flowers in a vase we delivered to Nesta's room at the hospital, where he lay bedridden after his operation.

Nesta fought back from the operation until he had enough feeble strength left to go back to the rented house. When he was moved, I took the heart out of the vase as a keepsake.

I have Rita's plastic heart with me unto this very day.

Chapter Thirteen

It was no secret that Nesta had other women in his life and that many of them bore him children and me grandchildren. In this, he was not unusual. Rastas are believers in scripture, which instructs us to go forth, be fruitful and multiply. Indeed, so common in Jamaica is the practice of bearing children out of wedlock that a woman who does it is called a baby-mother, and the man a baby-father, with no apostrophe 's'.

Nesta died leaving one widow, seven baby-mothers, and eleven children who would eventually be recognized by the court as heirs to his estate. Only three were his by Rita: Cedella, Ziggy and Steve. But all these children, my grandchildren – whether born in or out of wedlock – I regarded then and now as Jah's blessings.

Cindy Breakspeare, who was crowned Miss World in 1976, bore him Damian. Janet in Jamaica gave him Rohan, whom I adopted and who made a name for himself as a linebacker for the Miami Hurricanes' championship football team. Janet in England gave him Karen, who was raised by Rita. Pat bore Robbie, Anita had Kimani, and Lucy in England had Julian. Rita's child by Ital, Stephanie, was also an heir to the estate, as was Makada, whose mother was Yvette. Jennifer got pregnant for Nesta but lost the baby. Winnie bore him no children.

Also involved with Nesta was Pascalene, the daughter of the President of Gabon. She turned out to be one of his most caring and loving women, sticking with him to the bitter end even after his sickness had turned him back into a helpless baby. Diane Jobson may have been more than Nesta's lawyer, best friend and confidante, but if so, I don't know. Nevertheless, a truer, more loving heart than Diane's Nesta never knew while he walked this earth. She was present at his deathbed.

These are the women I knew. There were no doubt others I didn't know.

Nesta himself introduced me to many of the women who bore him children, and after his passing I grew to know them all at the various court hearings. But I observed up-close his relationship with two women in particular: Cindy and Yvette.

In her prime, Cindy was strikingly good-looking and athletic, and even before she was crowned Miss World, was known throughout Jamaica as a stunning beauty.

The first time I heard her name mentioned was when Nesta was staying with me in Delaware, where he'd stopped over on his way from England. He called Cindy in Jamaica and after chatting briefly, handed me the phone. For a few minutes, Cindy and I exchanged pleasantries.

After Mr Booker had passed, Nesta, who by then had made it big in the music world, bought me a lovely home in Coral Gables, south of Miami, where he lived with me when he was not on tour or recording. One day he told me that Cindy was coming from Jamaica to visit, and a little bit later she showed up and we finally met face to face.

She was every bit as good-looking in real life as she was in her pictures and had a strong voice, not high-pitched or shrill like you might expect from a beauty queen. On this visit, she and Nesta spent hours romping in the pool, splashing and having fun. Soon afterwards she got pregnant and later gave birth to Damian.

Cindy was a stern mother who raised her son with discipline. One time, for example, when she was staying here with me, she and Nesta went out and I was left to care for the baby. Cindy was emphatic that once she had put the baby down for the night, I was not to lift him out of the crib or go to him if he cried, for that was the way she was breaking him.

I said, fine, if that was what she wanted – it was, she stressed – and thankfully, my grandmother's instincts were not put to the temptation, since the baby simply lay on the bed gurgling, staring around the room, and a few minutes later, just as Cindy had said he would, fell sound asleep.

When it became known throughout Jamaica that Nesta was involved with Cindy, people began to talk. Cindy was an uptown girl from the posh suburbs of St Andrew, Nesta was seen as a ghetto youth, and in some people's minds, there were impossible barriers of race and class between them. Rita, for example, used to refer to Cindy as 'a white woman'.

This was during the stormy seventies, the fretful times of Michael Manley's socialism. In those fiery days of black against white, poor against rich, up against down, and front against back, that Nesta should get involved with a fair-skinned girl like Cindy caused a scandal on both sides of the street. Up the road or down the road, everyone in Kingston was talking about their love affair. Public opinion was heatedly against it.

One time, for example, I was with Rita and Peter Tosh in Jamaica, and the two of them began chatting about Nesta and Cindy. In strong, hot-blooded words, Peter raged against a Rasta brother getting involved with a white woman. He told us he intended to go straight up to 56 Hope Road, where Nesta lived, and speak his mind openly on the subject.

Rita and I left Peter and went about our business up and down Kingston, but later we met him again at Half-Way-Tree, and he told us that he was on his way to have it out with Nesta and Cindy.

Arriving at 56 Hope Road ahead of him, I went to warn Nesta

that Peter and an explosion were ahead. 'Peter fussing?' was all Nesta asked, looking amused.

A few minutes later Peter walked into the yard as meek as a lamb. There was no outburst, no fussing, no thunderbolts, not even a pop-gun or fire-cracker. He had some music business to discuss with Nesta, and the two of them huddled in a corner and talked.

When he was done, Peter blew softly out the gate – like a night breeze.

If the Rasta brethren didn't approve of Nesta and Cindy, neither did her own family.

I caught my first glimpse of the family's discontent one day shortly after Damian was born. Nesta dropped me off at Cindy's, and I glimpsed her mother in the yard as I entered the house to visit my newest grandson.

After I'd visited and kitchy-cooed the infant Damian, Cindy said she'd introduce me to her mother, but when she looked, the lady had left without saying a word. I felt a vibe. Embarrassed, Cindy took me to see her craft shop, which occupied a small building right in front of her house – a house that Nesta had bought her.

On another occasion Cindy invited me over to lunch. We ate in the kitchen, and I finally got to meet her mother.

'I notice when I came here de odder day,' I remarked to her, 'you tried to avoid me.'

'I never tried to avoid you,' she sputtered.

'Yes, you did. You left as soon as I came.'

She looked flustered. 'To tell you de truth,' she said, 'Cindy has a baby for your son, and yet he has Rita, too.'

'Well, you know,' I replied, 'Nesta married to Rita.'

'What?' she exclaimed. 'I didn't know dat!'

'I don't believe you,' I shot back. 'Because everything Nesta does come out in de newspaper.'

Cindy, who was standing nearby listening, chimed in, 'Yes, I heard dat Bob was married. But he never admitted it to me.'

'Well,' I said, 'dat's Nesta. But he's married. And to Rita.'

Cindy's mother fumed and looked vexed.

'I don't mind having Bob's children,' Cindy said coolly. 'I love children. I'd like to have about ten of dem.'

'Bob wants to have his cake and eat it too,' grumbled Cindy's mother. She complained that when Cindy lived at 56 Hope Road with Nesta, he would not come into a room where the mother was, and sometimes if she entered a room where he was, he would immediately get up and leave. I explained to her that Nesta was shy and that Mr Booker had lodged the very same complaint.

'Is respect him showing you,' I added.

She sniffed, obviously not happy that her glamorous, beautiful daughter was, as Jamaicans would say, Nesta's 'boops', meaning his woman on the side.

I told them both that Nesta was a man, and a man will always be a man, and that just because a man does something doesn't mean that the woman should do it too. I don't think this opinion sat well with the mother, but we parted with at least a little better understanding between us.

With Nesta's life bound up so openly with all these women, it was inevitable that sooner or later awkward moments would catch up with him. Such a moment happened one day to Rita and Cindy.

One time Cindy was staying with Nesta at my house in Miami when Rita suddenly phoned to say that she was flying in with the children for a visit. Panicked, Cindy wondered if she should leave, but I assured her that it was all right, that Rita would not make a scene.

Rita and Nesta were then living apart – she in Bull Bay and Nesta at 56 Hope Road. Plus, Rita had Ital on the side, although she was still then trying to hide him from Nesta. Yet as soon as Rita arrived, Nesta left his bed with Cindy in it and slept with his children on the sofa or on the carpeted floor of the drawing-room. Everyone was civilized and conversational at the breakfast and dinner table, and if there was tension between the two women – the lawful wife and beauty queen mistress – it didn't show.

But Cindy must have felt uncomfortable with the arrangement, especially since she had been left alone in Nesta's bed now that his wife and children were under the same roof. A day or so later she departed, for she could see that while his children were present, out of respect for them, Nesta would not share his bed with her, especially not right under Rita's nose.

There were other fusses, too.

One day Cindy came and asked me if I thought it was right for Nesta to lie to her. I asked her what he'd lied about, and she said she'd heard that he'd bought Rita a brand-new BMW for her birthday.

'And here my VW Beetle is barely running,' she added bitterly.

I advised her not to quarrel about it because, after all, Rita and Nesta were man and wife with three children between them.

'But he lied to me!' she fumed.

'How?'

'I asked him if he'd bought Rita a car and he said, "De woman buy her own car." And dat's a lie!'

I sighed. In such an argument, a mother had no use. Puss don't business in dog fight.

Yet even though things were cordial on the surface, Rita still felt hurt over Cindy. I myself witnessed this hurt in her when Nesta was on tour in California.

I'd baked a cake for Nesta and was going to send it to him with a friend who was joining the tour the next day. But the man offered to buy me an airline ticket so he would have company on the long flight to California, and at the urging of my other children, I went.

I checked into the hotel where the band was staying and roomed with Rita. The next morning when I awoke, Rita was already gone.

I got up, dressed, and went and knocked on Nesta's door. Rita answered. She was weeping openly.

'What wrong with you?' I asked.

She hurried into the bathroom and closed the door without answering. Inside, Nesta was sprawled out on the bed.

'Hello, Nesta,' I said.

'A wa' a gwan?' he said, using the patois Jamaican greeting that means, 'What's going on?'

Later, I found that I'd caught them in the middle of their recurring quarrel over Stephanie. Nesta had been pressing Rita to admit that the child was not his and to name the real father. Rita had been stubbornly refusing to admit anything although later, on this very day, she would finally confirm Nesta's worse fears by naming Ital as Stephanie's father. I'd come in right in the middle of this muggle-muggle.

I said, 'Me hear Cindy have baby.' In fact, I'd gotten the news only that morning.

'Yeah. Dat's why Rita a cry and go on so,' Nesta said.

'Oh, yeah?'

'You know,' he said bitterly, 'it take Rita three years to admit de truth 'bout Stephanie. Three years.'

I could hear Rita's muffled sobs coming from the bathroom.

'Well,' he continued, 'me no want anodder man to raise my children. And since me not going live wid Rita, me no know how it goin' go.'

A few minutes later, when I returned to my own room, Rita walked in and muttered something about visioning that I'd come to her house and taken Nesta's children. I assured her that she'd had a false vision, that her children were her own, not mine, and that they were hers to raise.

All this bickering and confusion took place in a luxury hotel in California. That night, amidst all this upheaval, Rita and Nesta would appear on stage, and sing their hearts out to adoring fans.

Pressure. Pressure. And more pressure.

Then there was Yvette, whom Nesta met in California.

Yvette was a radio DJ in Berkeley, California, and a former girlfriend of Johnny Nash when Nesta got involved with her. She was a fair-skinned woman from Philadelphia, very fidgety and with 'nuff mouth. She began visiting me regularly in Delaware, sometimes when Nesta was present, sometimes when he was gone on tour. When Nesta was home, she spent the night in his bed. When he was away, she stayed by herself in a guest room. For the most part, I didn't mind having her around, for she was lively, funny, chatty, and loved to laugh. With her bright spirit, she gave me good companionship.

Then she and Nesta suddenly fell out. Nesta was done with Yvette, but Yvette was not done with me: she grabbed and held on to me like a crab. She wrote often, long letters of three, four sheets. She called regularly. Nesta would return from touring and see her letters lying around and ask, 'A wa Yvette a write you 'bout now?' I heard her life story several times and in many versions – over the phone, through the mail, face to face.

Around this time we had moved to Miami and found that Nesta was getting so much fan mail that we had to set up a system for answering the letters. But Nesta didn't want to start a fan club – he said that sounded too fanny-fanny and egotistical – so we founded the Movement of Jah People as an organization for handling the mail from fans.

Yvette struck me as the perfect choice to help me with the

correspondence. She had public relations experience. As a former DJ, she knew Nesta's music well. Moreover, she was used to dealing with the public. I called and asked her if she'd like to come to Miami and work for the Movement of Jah People, and she eagerly agreed. She said she was on her way to visit Johnny Nash at his horse farm and would come by afterwards. Soon she was living under my roof and working for the Movement of Jah People.

Nesta, however, showed no further interest in Yvette as a woman. He would be in and out, depending on his recording or touring schedule, and she would be up and about the house as an employee, handling the correspondence from Nesta's fans all over the world. Their footsteps would criss-cross in the drawing-room, kitchen and patio, but his bedroom door remained closed to her.

Everything was proceeding more or less smoothly, except that every now and again Yvette and her 'nuff mouth would rude off to me and I'd have to teach her manners by boxing her face. One day, for example, I asked Yvette to phone the dentist and make an appointment for me. Later that afternoon she was driving me somewhere in my Cadillac when I asked her if she'd remembered to call the dentist. In reply, she gave me a faisty answer, asking me if I thought the phone's cord was tied to her – and she said the nasty *p* word.

'What!' I cried, unable to believe my ears. 'Who you talking to?' I leaned over and boxed her on the side of her face. I was immediately sorry, for I had on a ring with a pointed tip, and it left a red pock-mark in her skin.

When I hit her, she jumped a mile, burst into tears, and rammed my Cadillac into the embankment with a jolt.

'Is so you try fe mash up me car?' I yelled at her. 'Get out! Get outta me car right now!'

She jumped out of the car and slammed the door. I slid over to the driver's seat and drove myself home.

A few minutes later Yvette came to the house and said she wanted to remove her things.

'Pack up everything you own and get out of my house,' I barked at her.

She made a great fuss as if she were taking down her clothes off the hangers, but taking down nothing, as if pulling clothes out of the drawer, but pulling out nothing, while I sat and watched.

The next thing I knew I saw a strapping uniformed man looming over me in my own hallway.

'But wait!' I exclaimed. 'Is no policeman dis?'

In the background, I glimpsed another officer, lurking by the front door.

'What you doing here, officer?' I asked.

He replied that they'd had a report from one Yvette that a lady in this house was fighting and beating her.

'Now, officer?' I asked him sweetly. 'Look 'pon me, poor old woman, and dis ya young gal. You think me could fight dis? You think me would beat dis?'

Puzzled, the officer looked from me to Yvette, then turned sharply on his heels and snapped to his partner, 'Come on, Eddy,' and the two of them climbed into their patrol car and drove away.

'Yvette,' I said to her, 'why you bring policeman inna me house?'

She burst into tears and began one loud piece of hysterical wailing and sobbing. 'Look at your eyes!' she howled, trembling. 'Look at your eyes!' She was cowering before me as if she was about to throw herself down in front of me and beg mercy.

'You wait till Bob come!' I told her. 'You wait till I tell him dat you bring policeman to me house.'

Later, everything settled down and was forgiven, and we resumed working together on the Movement of Jah People.

Yvette had moved into an apartment, where she could receive

her own visitors. She had one boyfriend whose name was Vincent and who used to come and visit her, and another nicknamed LA, a young but manly boy, who was madly in love with her. Yvette, too, was smitten with the boy. Once I overheard her asking her mother if she thought the boy was too young for her to marry.

One Saturday, Yvette came by and invited Nesta to come and see her new apartment. The two of them drove off in Yvette's car.

The weeks flew past. Nesta went on tour. Then he collapsed in Central Park and the diagnosis fell on us like a terrible judgment: the cancer in his toe had spread to his brain. There was no hope. Nesta fell into a long and painful dying.

One day during the unbearable heaviness of my grief, I rang Yvette. Sobbing, she said she couldn't talk, but she'd call back. She called back a few minutes later, still sobbing, to blurt out, after some wailing and gnashing of teeth, that she was pregnant.

'Fe who?'

'I think is for Bob.'

'Go 'way, gal, you lie!'

'I'm not sure. I have to check my diary.'

'You do dat.'

She checked; she came back with the same story. The child was Nesta's; it was due on 11 May according to her. She said the conception had happened on the day she'd taken Nesta to see her new apartment.

At Nesta's request, I went to Germany to care for him during his sickness, and when I got there I told him what Yvette had said. He remarked that she hadn't told him that the child was his, she'd only said that she was pregnant. I promised him that if the child was his, I would care for it. Then we moved on to other things, for he was suffering terrible pain.

Two weeks after Nesta passed, Yvette brought her newborn baby she had named Makada to show me. It was a beautiful child, a healthy, bubbling daughter.

Yvette moved to Philadelphia and disappeared for a while. The squabbling over the estate had begun. I found myself fighting to keep the roof over my head, as the house that Nesta had given me was in danger of being taken away by the administrators of the estate.

When Yvette phoned again, she was in a hysterical mood, weeping that her baby was hungry and that she would have to go on welfare, for she had no other means of support. I angrily told her not to take Nesta's name down to the welfare office, and I agreed to help her with some temporary support until it could be proved that the child was really Nesta's.

Soon Yvette had hired a lawyer who submitted an application to the administrators of the estate, claiming that she had borne Nesta a child who should be numbered among his heirs. Rita refused to sign the papers acknowledging Nesta's fatherhood. Yvette took a blood test, but the results were inconclusive: anyone could be the father. As Jamaicans say, 'Death cut words'; Nesta could no longer speak for himself.

Yet, with Yvette still yapping in my ears over the telephone, begging scraps for her newborn, I realized that there was an innocent involved, a child born into a world where adults were quarreling over her past, her paternity, her future.

I consented to sign the paper admitting Nesta's paternity of the infant.

Rita had little to do with Yvette, before or after Nesta's passing. Yvette was simply one more woman in Nesta's life, one more annoyance to Rita, one more pinprick of jealousy. And as I said, when the dispute about Nesta's paternity of Makada came up, Rita flatly refused to sign the papers admitting the child as a claimant to the estate. Instead, she brought the papers to me and said, 'You do what you think is right, Mom. You were dere. I wasn't.'

And for the child's sake, I did sign the papers.

Nevertheless, even though Rita never came into the same kind of jealous conflict with Yvette that she suffered with Cindy, I remember one conversation I overheard between Nesta and Rita that summed up the many complications that came between them and lasted until the final separation caused by death. Rita was then expecting Stephanie, conceived while Nesta was away working in England.

When Nesta returned from England, he found that Bunny and Peter didn't want to tour any more because they were tired of flying, and he needed to find someone else to back him up. (This someone else would later turn out to be the I-Threes.) He phoned Rita and they had a long, long chat.

Somehow, I don't know how, a rumor had started that Nesta planned to marry Yvette to get his permanent US papers, and word had gotten back to Rita's ears. For his part, Nesta was suspicious about Rita's latest pregnancy.

The exchange, as I gathered from listening to Nesta, went something like this.

'So, me hear seh you going marry a white woman,' Rita said.

'So me no hear you seh you breeding. Who de baby-father?'

'You tell her you already married, or you keeping it secret?'

'Me in England working, and you in Jamaica breeding baby. So who de baby-father? Tell me, nuh? Why you hiding it?'

'Man can't marry two woman at once, you know. Dem will lock you up.'

'Married woman not supposed to breed when a husband no de a yard. You don't know dat?'

Nesta eventually got tired of this back-and-forth chatter and handed me the telephone.

'Me hear you son goin' marry one white woman,' Rita quipped.

'To who?'

'How you mean, to who? Maybe right now even as you and me talking, de gal might be dere listening.'

And in this, Rita was partly right: Yvette was at my house then, spending time with Nesta.

But she was not listening.

Chapter Fourteen

Nesta's success in the music world could have gone to his head and drawn him away from his roots and family. Such a story is common – the young man who becomes a great success and quickly forgets where he came from and who brought him into this world now that he has gone up on high.

But that was the way of someone else's son, not my Nesta. His success did not cause him to forget his roots, but bound him ever closer to them. Even as the world exalted him, he remained as humble as ever and drew still closer to me.

Jamaican men, on the whole, tend to stay close to their mothers all throughout life. In fact, years ago there was a popular calypso on this theme – I forget who sang it or the exact words – but it went something like this:

> *If you modder and you wife were drowning*
> *which one would you save?*

The calypsonian then sings some funny lyrics about the two main women in his life – his mother and his wife – before the refrain of the song speaks his heart plainly:

> *I can always get another wife,*
> *but you modder is you modder*
> *for all you life.*

Of course, not every Jamaican man feels this way, but many

do. I only know that during his lifetime, Nesta never forgot his mother.

In fact, I remember one day as Rita and I were strolling through the garden talking, as we often did, Nesta came up to us and asked what we were chatting about. We said nothing in particular, we were just looking at the flowers and the plants.

'If me modder and me wife was drowning,' Nesta said mischievously, quoting the song, 'I wonder which one me woulda save.'

'Save we both!' Rita laughed.

Nesta chuckled and wandered away, leaving me and Rita alone to continue on our garden stroll.

Even as the world adored him, Nesta remained steadfast and strong in his loyalty and love for his roots and the family that had raised him to manhood.

With the world now showering him with praise and wealth, radio stations playing his songs that frequently hit the charts, magazines writing articles about him and his life, television reporters begging for interviews, Nesta made sure that I shared in his new-found but hard-earned prosperity. When he was away recording or on tour, every now and again he would send a check for $500 or $1000 from England without being asked. When he was visiting me or I was visiting him, he would often just walk up and hand me a bundle of money, saying, 'Mamma, see some money here.'

With Nesta's help, I bought four houses and a barber shop in Delaware, all as investments. Unfortunately, all of them turned out to be money-losers.

The first house I bought was from an old lady named Miss Dixon, who lived beside me and had come down with a wicked case of the shingles. While she was sick, I cut her grass, took care of her yard, and sat at her sickbed when I could, to give her comfort. She used to urge me to buy her house, and when her only son decided to take her in, I told Nesta that there was a place available right beside mine. The purchase price was small – some $3000 or $4000 – a figure at which Nesta marveled, 'A so little de house selling for?'

Shortly afterwards, he sent up the money with Rita, and I bought the house. It became Nesta's place to stay when he was visiting me in Delaware.

Rita was similarly generous now that she and Nesta had become rich. I never parted company with Rita without her giving me money, even if it was only candy money. When I visited Rita in Bull Bay, I never came down off her hilltop without her stuffing dollar bills in my pocket.

However, on the occasion when Rita brought up the check from Jamaica to buy Miss Dixon's house, she was snappy-snappy with me and acting so faisty that I even said to her, 'Is who you talking to like dat? Wait! When Nesta come, I going tell him you action here today, for I know he wouldn't appreciate it.'

It was not a serious quarrel, just what you would call a mouth-meet, meaning a family tiff. Later the cause of her cross mood became clear when Carmen, my brother Gibson's wife, rode on the plane back to Jamaica with Rita. When she returned to Delaware, Carmen told me that Rita had been nauseous and throwing up during the whole trip. She was pregnant with Stephanie.

My investments in property always happened after I had a vision of cleaning an old house. Once I had this vision, I would know that an opportunity to invest in a property was upcoming. When the opportunity arose, I'd discuss it with Nesta, and he would willingly supply the funds. This was how he bought me a barber shop, providing every penny of the purchase price.

'See it ya, now, Mamma,' he said on that occasion. 'Me going buy you dis shop. Now all you have to do is go collect you rent.'

It was around this time and during these transactions that I discovered how strongly Nesta was against wills. Since he'd put up the money for these property investments, I always recorded Nesta as the legal owner of the places I bought. And because our business was so mixed up, I wanted to clarify in my will his rightful ownership of the properties.

Nesta objected. 'Me no business inna will,' he protested. 'No put me name down inna any will.'

'But de old must dead one day, Nesta,' I argued, 'and de business between us must be clear or contention goin' come up.'

'No, Mamma!' he insisted. 'No put me name inna no will.'

I went to the lawyer and told him of my son's objections, and he said he would find a way to protect Nesta's interests even if he didn't give his name outright in the will.

I'm not sure what the lawyer did, but whatever it was quieted Nesta's fears and nothing further was said on the subject.

Nesta never loved material goods. As a devout Rasta and an avid reader of the Bible, he knew and could recite by heart many scripture verses that warn against the love of wealth, such as, 'If riches increase, lay not your heart upon it.' The one in his family who loved the material world was not Nesta, but Rita. To Nesta, great wealth was little more than another of the world's empty playthings.

One time, for example, I remember Nesta asking Diane Jobson how much money he had in his various bank accounts, for he didn't have the vaguest idea. Diane made some telephone calls – his accounts were then worldwide – and handed him a paper on which she had scribbled down some figures. Nesta glanced at the numbers without changing expression. Then he crumpled the paper and threw it in the wastepaper basket.

At the time, he was worth millions, most of it in cash deposits. But he gave no sign of gladness or rejoicing. For all I could tell from his expression, Diane might have scribbled down $20 on the paper, instead of the string of fish-eye zerocs that bespoke his millions.

Even after he had become rich and famous, Nesta not only remained faithful and true to his Rasta faith, but also continued to be modest and unassuming in all his dealings with people. He did not puff up his heart and think himself better or more blessed than his fellow-creatures. Instead, true to himself and his nature, he remained shy and humble.

One time, for example, shortly after Nesta had released the album *Exodus*, he was with me in Delaware when a group of the brethren came down from Philadelphia to visit. We were all in the living-room of his house reasoning and listening to the joyful music when a lady named Betty Smith, who was the barber then renting the shop that Nesta had bought me, stopped by and asked if she could come in and say hello to him. I said, certainly, she was welcome.

She entered the room timidly, shook hands with Nesta and marveled at the sight of his powerful, flowing locks.

'Bob,' she giggled, 'what that you have on you head? Is hair?'

Locks were then rarer than today and seldom was seen a head so full of strong and mighty ones as Nesta then sported.

'Of course is hair,' Nesta said.

'Can I feel it?'

'Yes, you can feel it, so long as is not in a mockery way.'

The woman was obviously under the false impression that people often have about locks – that they were coarse and dirty, which is far from the truth. She reached over and stroked Nesta's dreadlocks, touching them with respect and reverence.

'Oh, my God!' she exclaimed. 'This is incredible. It's so soft!'

Nesta just sat on the couch, looked up at her, and smiled.

Faced with that kind of daily glorification, a weaker man would have had his head turned and been tempted to strut up and down like a bull in a backyard pen gloating over his three or four timid cows. But Nesta was not puffed up and vain; if anything, he was only amused.

Years later, after Nesta had passed, I was in New York when Roger Steffens, a friend of mine, brought some locks in a paper bag and asked if I believed they could have come from Nesta's head. He said that they were just handed to him by a man claiming to have found them in the closet of a house once occupied by Nesta.

'Throw away dat piece o' dutty something,' I told him impatiently. 'Where dis boy fe go get Bob locks?'

Even today at reggae festivals, if you look weak-minded enough to these jinals (con-men), they'll slink out of the shadows, whisper 'Psssst!' and try and sell you what they'll swear are pieces of Nesta's dreadlocks. But which part of the donkey or goat or mule or sheep, or which criminal head that bogus hair comes from, is known only to Jah.

Although Nesta was my son, in spiritual matters he grew to become my father and teacher. The babe and suckling ended up being the teacher of his mother.

It was Nesta who showed me the truth and put my aging feet on the path of righteousness. It was the son who taught the mother that the biblical patriarchs of yore – Moses, Solomon, David, Jesus – were black one and all, and that the world had passed down to the generations the lie that these holy men had been white.

Nesta taught me of the divinity of Haile Selassie I, Emperor of Ethiopia and most holy son of Jah, who walked the earth like a humble and ordinary man but who was the living and true Godhead in the flesh. Nesta taught me that Haile Selassie was descended from the tribe of David and the seed of Jesse, that His great-ancestor was Solomon, that His was the living presence of Jah among men.

Man read it, and man know it, said Nesta. Everybody know

that Haile Selassie I is God. Even the Pope knew it. But in its vanity and pride, the world stubbornly refused to admit the truth, that a black God was earth's rightful ruler.

It was Nesta who saved my life by teaching me about ganja, the herb that Rastas use to find the way to enlightenment, the wisdom weed found growing wild on the grave of that wisest of patriarchs, Solomon.

Nesta explained to me that a lot of people have education to balance up themselves and show them right from wrong. Herb, Nesta showed me, was the poor man's education – it helped calm his nerves and relax his body, so that he could think on par with the man who could drink wisdom from a book. Nesta said that herbs energized the body and opened up the mind to thinking good and positive thoughts, that it contributed to the healing of nations. He said that ganja was good for many ailments, that if a child had a chest cold, a little herb boiled in water and sipped as a tea would clear up all congestion and make the sick one again draw a breath that was free and sweet.

All these things I proved myself long after Nesta had explained the principle and truth behind them to me. Late in life, for example, I came down suddenly with glaucoma. The eye doctor who treated me was worried: I could go blind, he said, for this was a wicked and dread disease that stole light from the eye. By then I had converted and been baptized a Rasta and was using the herb regularly as Rastas are instructed to do in daily worship.

Some months ran past. I visited the doctor again, and he shone his blue light into my eye and looked: no glaucoma, he said, pushing away his instruments. Something was wrong – glaucoma didn't just go away like that. Come back in three months for another examination.

Three months came and went. Another examination: no glaucoma. Come back again in six months.

Six months later: no glaucoma.

One year later: no glaucoma.

Two, three, four years later: no glaucoma. Herb had uprooted the disease from my eye and saved my sight.

From Nesta I learned the true story of Cain and Abel: that Cain lusted after his sister, whose favorite had been Abel. In a rage of jealousy, Cain slew Abel, and knew his sister.

But no crime on this earth, then or now, is unknown to Jah who, when He beheld this murder of brother by brother, cursed Cain, turned him white, and cast him out from among his own. Thus began the race of white men on the earth.

Nesta also taught me, and I myself have come to believe this truth, that everybody in the world, no matter what his color or the shape of his eye, belongs to Jah, as children belong to one father. Jah doesn't love me more, because of my black skin, than He loves another whose skin may be white. Nor does Jah love me any less. Jah loves all His children equally; His love is on one level. Jah says, he that cometh unto me, I will in no wise cast out. Love has no color, and the love of Jah knows no bounds, whether of geography, age, sex, or pigmentation of skin.

Since Nesta passed, I have traveled to Germany on many occasions to attend festivals held in his memory, meeting there many white Rastas who believe in and accept Jah, who sport full dreadlocks, who use the herb as the way to enlightenment. At one festival, they presented me with an ancient handmade Bible written in Amharic, printed on parchment, and with a decorative cover hard like wood. They cooked Ital food for me and brought me plates of steaming vegetables and sweet fruit. In my discussions with these white brethren, I discovered that many of them, although living the simple and pure life of Rasta, are well-educated men and women, not boobikiah (stupid people).

These white Rastas follow the teachings of the faith. Living pure and natural, they avoid all flesh-eating, shun the politricks of worldly governments, cast aside all cravings for the material world, and instead spend their days to the full in spiritual contemplation. They are the sons and daughters of Jah, no less and no more than their black brothers and sisters in Jamaica, in America, in England, in the motherland of Africa, throughout all the four corners of the world that are known and charted by Babylonian geographers.

Nesta taught me about hair and dreadlocks. He showed me how a Rasta should cause his hair to grow free and wild, not to allow either comb or razor to disturb its natural progress. He taught me that locks are a source of spiritual and physical strength such as Samson – the biblical black man of power and might – was said to possess.

All this, and more, I learned, sitting at the feet of my first-begotten son. In the beginning I resisted, because my heart had been hardened by the Babylonian teachings and mentality in my upbringing. But over the years my heart began to melt and soften, and I beheld the truth.

My conversion to Rasta came to me in a vision. I was then involved in dealings with a bishop of the Pentecostal Church, and the man proved himself to be a thief.

I had hired him to do some renovations of my house, only to find that the Babylonian wretch was overcharging me for materials. There was a dispute and his wickedness was revealed in its fullness.

I had become involved in that particular church because Bishop Brown, my sister Ivy's husband, had been its head. Then Bishop Brown met in an accident and died, and his high seat was captured by this man. When I discovered the man's wickedness, I told him that as long as I lived, he could not preach to me from a pulpit, for he was a wretch.

'Sister Ciddy,' he sputtered, 'you talking to me like that?'

'You lucky is just talk me a talk,' I raged.

Shortly afterwards, I had a vision. I visioned that I went to the church, and I walked right up to the rostrum where the thief stood, preparing to preach. Looking on, the whole congregation was respectfully seated and assembled in worship.

'Bishop,' I announced loudly before one and all, 'I coming out of this church and I going over to Bob.'

'But, Sister Ciddy,' he protested lamely, 'I thought you and me were going to do some business.'

'No,' I replied, 'you and me going do no business whatsoever, for I am now going over to Bob.'

Then I woke up out of my sleep.

That next morning I was telling my sister Ivy and brother David my vision, interpreting it to mean that I would convert to Rasta. Both strongly objected.

'A backslide you backsliding,' my brother charged.

'Better to backslide to somewhere than frontslide to nowhere,' I replied.

My mind was made up. From that moment on I would be Rasta. I would take to heart the command of Jah, 'Take my yoke upon you and learn of me. My yoke is easy and my burden is light.'

I would have done with Babylonian hypocrisy.

All Jah asks of his brethren is a clean hand and a pure heart, not observances of stupid and petty rules and regulations of Babylonian hypocrisy, where one thing is preached within the walls of the church and another practiced outside in shameful view of Jah's sunshine and moonlight. I would heed Jah's words and love my brother, for the greatest of Jah's commandments is love. I would henceforth drown my brother in my love. I would be Rasta.

I changed the eating habits of the family, causing a little struggle between me and Mr Booker, for I swore off all flesh of the swine, telling him about ham that, 'It nah come in ya, and me nah cook it.' I gave up most flesh-eating and began feeding my family mainly wholesome vegetarian dishes.

Mr Booker, who loved his picnic ham and his bacon, would sigh and go off elsewhere to eat his swine meat. But none of it would touch the lips of me or my children.

In 1978, around the time of the famous peace concert held in the National Stadium on Mountain View Avenue in Kingston where Nesta brought together the warring Edward Seaga of the Jamaica Labour Party (JLP) and Michael Manley of the People's National Party (PNP), I was baptized by Abba, a priest in the Ethiopian Orthodox Church, and given the baptismal name Aklilleworqe, meaning 'The Golden Crown'. Nesta's baptismal name had been Berhane Selassie, meaning 'Light of the Trinity'.

In name and in creed, both of us were now Rastas. The son had taken the mother by the hand, and shown her the light, the truth, the road. For this alone, I will always honor and bless my son's soul and memory.

Chapter Fifteen

There are some years when trouble prowls outside your window like a thief, scratching to break into your life. You hear the sounds of unknown footsteps in the night; you hear creaks and tell-tale noises of breakage; you lie on your bed, huddled under the sheets in the darkness, listening to the pounding of your heart and feeling helpless.

That was how I was during the dark years of the late 1970s when trouble, a thief armed with a machete, stalked outside my window.

One morning in February 1976, a crisp winter day in Delaware, I awoke, looked at Mr Booker's face lying across from me on the bed, and saw on it the stamp of death.

Mr Booker was a steadfast Baptist, unswerving in his faith and in his good deeds to his congregation and church, never narrow-minded about his religion as a lesser man with a Jamaican wife lately converted to Rastafarianism might have been. If Mr Booker had an appetite for animal flesh, he ate it at the house of his own mother. He never criticized my religion or Nesta's, never made an unkind remark against His Majesty, never spoke a harsh word against my newfound beliefs that had radically changed his daily diet. Mr Booker worshipped a white god, Nesta and I a black one, but even faced with such strong differences, Mr Booker never raised a cross word against us.

'I have nothing bad to say against Bob and his religion,' Mr

Booker told me one day. 'Every man on this earth worship the same God, no matter if they call him by a different name or give him a different color.'

That was Mr Booker: always calm, tolerant and reasonable in his outlook.

On the morning that I saw death in his face, Mr Booker was being harassed by members of his congregation because there was no heat in the church building. The night before one of them had called up to complain that the furnace was broken and the church cold. I'd gotten snappy with the fellow, for even though Mr Booker was the caretaker of the church, lately he hadn't been feeling well and had been complaining of a terrible weariness.

'What you have dis old man running up and down de place for, eh?' I had said sharply to the brother who had called to complain. 'What is wrong with you people? You hand join church?'

'Hand join church' is a Jamaican expression that signifies idleness, meaning that the person's hand serves no more useful labor than pointless church clapping.

The man did not understand me. He kept yapping about the church being cold.

When he awoke that morning with death stamped on his face, Mr Booker had just suffered through a double dose of worries the night before. First, he'd been pestered by the congregation; second, my niece had come crying on my doorstep because her estranged husband had just smashed down her kitchen door and stabbed her with an ice-pick. Bleeding from the stabbing, she had begged Mr Booker to accompany her home – for she was afraid to go there alone – survey the damage and call the police.

So Mr Booker, already burdened by a cold church, arose out of his warm bed and trudged a few doors down the street in the bitter cold, to get involved in a violent domestic dispute.

By the time he returned from the police station where he'd

gone to file charges against the boy who'd stabbed my niece, it was nearly one o'clock in the morning. I heard him climb into the bed beside me and snuggle down under the blanket with a weary groan.

The next morning was when I saw the haggard look of death stamped on his features.

'Eddy,' I shook him, alarmed, 'why you look like dis? My God, you look like somebody dying or dead.'

'Ciddy,' Mr Booker moaned softly, 'I'm tired.'

Mr Booker crawled slowly out of his bed and went downstairs to make coffee and chat with a gentleman who was then living with us. When I joined them at the breakfast table, Mr Booker said to me, 'Ciddy, I'm not feeling good at all.'

'You should just stay home and rest up yourself,' I advised him.

'I can't,' he said wearily. 'I have to take the children to school. Then I have to look about heat in the church.'

At the time Nesta and Rita were touring, and their children were staying with me. Every morning Mr Booker had a carload of children, for he used to transport Cedella, Ziggy, Steve, Richard and Pearl to school.

Mr Booker left on his rounds, leaving me fixing breakfast. I kept waiting for him to return to eat breakfast with me, but he didn't appear at the usual hour.

The telephone rang: it was Mr Booker still at the church, asking if the workmen who were to repair the furnace had called. I said no, they hadn't, and he told me that if they should call, I was to send them to him immediately, for he was waiting to let them into the church.

I had two small children with me – my Anthony and another little boy I baby-sat for – and housekeeping chores to do, so the morning was flying past with the usual hustle-bustle.

Suddenly, the doorbell rang. Standing shivering at my front door was one of the workmen.

'What you doing here?' I began, 'Mr Booker waiting—'

'Mrs Booker,' he interrupted, 'I think something happen to your husband. I found him lying on the church floor.'

The man was a foreigner who spoke broken English with a strong accent, and at first I had trouble understanding him, but finally I grasped what he was trying to say: Mr Booker was sick. He was unconscious in the workman's car.

I raced outside without putting on a coat and, as a wicked cold licked me, found Mr Booker slumped unconscious in the back seat.

Water was drooling down his chin; his tongue dangled out of his mouth; his eyes had turned, and he was wringing-wet with sweat.

'Jesus almighty!' I cried.

I ran next door and begged a neighbor to watch the two small children at my house. Then we dashed off to the hospital with Mr Booker.

On the way, Mr Booker stirred and groaned.

'Eddy,' I begged him, 'don't give up on me! Please! Please! Please!'

I had grabbed a bottle of Bay rum from the medicine chest, and on the way I was rubbing Mr Booker with it to try and revive him, for this is a traditional Jamaican remedy used for all sickness. I fanned him; I massaged him; I rubbed his temples. He was limp and sweating and, no matter how frantically I fought to breathe life back into him, Mr Booker gave no sign of regaining consciousness.

When we got to the Wilmington Public Hospital, I ran inside, grabbed a passing nurse, and begged her to come outside and help me.

'What happened?' she asked.

'My husband is dying!' I cried frantically.

Following me to the car, she saw Mr Booker still slumped unconscious in the back seat. She ran inside and returned with

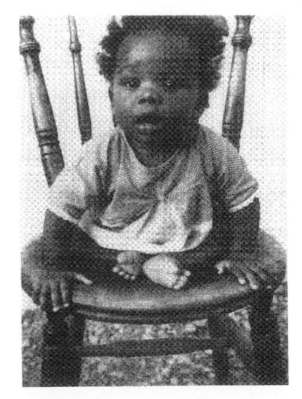

Above: A family gathering at Vista Lane, Miami, with Bob and myself. The children from left to right: Steve Marley, Cedella Marley, Ziggy Marley, Stephanie Marley, Robert Marley, Anthony Booker, Richard Booker

Right: My first grand-child, Cedella Marley

Above: Bob and his friends playing basketball in the Vista Lane yard. His son Ziggy is the youth just visible in the photograph

Below: Bob on the patio at Vista Lane with King Sporty and others

Above: The farmhouse where we lived near Dr Issels' clinic

Below: Inside the farm-house in Germany. From left to right: Seeco, Bob and Skill Cole

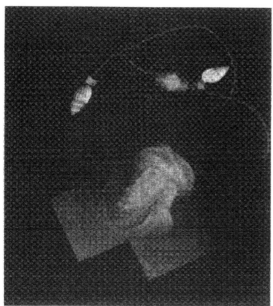

Above: Bob in Germany

Left: The cross from
the nurse who took care
of Bob and flew with us
back to Miami

Left: Bob's funeral (photograph: Kate Simon/Sygma)

Below: Bob's funeral reception, including, from left to right, Anthony Booker, Rita Marley, Ziggy Marley, Lucy Pounder, Steve Marley, Julian Marley, myself, Rohan Marley

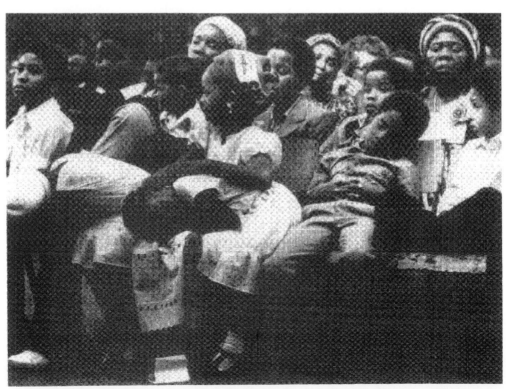

Above: Pascaline Bongo,
daughter of the President
of Gabon, during her first
visit to Jamaica

Above: Cindy Breakspeare
with her son Damian
Marley (my grandson)

Below: With Diane Jobson
in Jamaica

Above: With my grand-sons in Miami, 1996. From left to right: Steve Marley, Damian Marley, Julian Marley, Robert Marley, Rohan Marley, Ziggy Marley

Below: With Rita in Miami

Left: At 56 Hope Road,
Kingston (photograph:
Kate Simon/Sygma)

Below: Live at the
Lyceum (photograph:
Kate Simon/Sygma)

some other nurses, who spotted the bottle of Bay rum in the car. One of them asked suspiciously if Mr Booker had been drinking.

'No,' I said sharply. 'My husband don't drink.'

'So what is this?' she rejoined, holding up the bottle of Bay rum.

I explained that it was Bay rum, and that it is to us Jamaicans an all-purpose medicine, and that I was using it to rub his face to try and revive him.

Eventually, they believed me, put Mr Booker on a gurney, and rolled him into the hospital emergency room to be examined by a doctor.

When the doctor came to where I waited anxiously, he brought bad news: a blood vessel had burst in Mr Booker's brain. He'd had a stroke.

I felt dizzy. The doctor told me to put my head between my legs. He gave me something to smell.

'If he lives,' the doctor said grimly, after I'd regained my senses, 'he'll be a vegetable. There's nothing else you can do. Go home and come back later. We'll put him on a machine.'

That afternoon I returned to the hospital to find Mr Booker laid out on a bed in an upstairs room and hooked up to a machine. Every now and again the machine gave a violent shake like a wet dog and made a slapping sound followed by a hiss like it was gasping for breath.

I sat by Mr Booker's bed and whispered my goodbyes to this gentle, loving man.

'Oh, Eddy,' I said, 'you're such a good man. I know you can't talk, but you can hear me. God be with you, and God bless you.'

At three-thirty that afternoon, an hour or so after I'd returned home, the hospital phoned. Mr Booker had just died.

Mr Booker was dead; I was in mourning. My blood pressure, the same ailment that Mr Booker had suffered from, was skyrockcting. In November 1976, to settle my nerves, I decided to take a holiday and visit my Gen, Jane, in London.

The trip was a consoling break for me, my heart still heavy over Mr Booker's sudden death. I visited relatives and saw the sights, reveling in the excitement and stir of London life.

Early one morning the phone rang before the first dawn light was even seeping over the choppy rooftops of the city. It was Carl – Bunny's brother – calling from Wilmington.

'Miss Booker,' he said nervously, 'you son get shot.'

'What?' I cried, my heart suddenly racing.

'But is not serious,' he added hastily. 'Is not serious. Take it easy.'

'What happened?' I cried.

'Some people shot him up. Politics. But he's all right. Don't worry yourself 'bout dis. Him all right.'

Details of the attempted assassination were still sketchy – and remain so to this day – but I learned that Nesta's manager, Don Taylor, was seriously injured too with several bullet wounds. Rita had also been grazed in the head by the same gunmen.

I asked Carl about my other children, and he assured me that they were still in Delaware and just fine, that my sister Rose, whom I'd left in charge of them, said everyone was well.

I had a week left on my vacation, but remaining in England any longer was now impossible. I hurried home.

I found everything as I had left it: the children busy with school and their daily lives, the house intact, the world of Wilmington going about its usual business like a circus merry-go-round. But an air of uncertainty hung over our household because Nesta had disappeared from Jamaica after the shooting and no one knew where to find him. I waited for his call. He was said to have been shot, but not seriously wounded. But this information was mainly hearsay.

I'd reached home on a Friday afternoon. On Sunday, still

hung-over with jet-lag, I got up early, went downstairs in the quiet house, and prayed my heart out that Nesta would call and assure me that he was well. I prayed until the children were beginning to move about with the first light.

Then the phone rang: it was Nesta, calling from the Bahamas. 'Hi, Mamma,' he said.

'Jah Rastafarai!' I exclaimed joyfully. 'A you?'

'Yes, Mamma.'

'Oh, God!'

'Me all right, Mamma. Me all right!'

'Me was just praying to Jah to make me hear from you. Where you deh?'

'Me at Chris Blackwell house in de Bahamas.'

'All right. Me coming to see you tomorrow.'

'Come, nuh, Mamma. Come.'

The next day I flew down to the Bahamas, was met at the airport and driven to Chris's house.

Nesta was sitting with a group of companions in the backyard when I arrived, and he hurried over to embrace me. I burst into tears as we hugged.

'Nuh cry, Mamma,' he whispered, squeezing me tight. 'Nuh cry.'

'Me can't help meself,' I said through my tears. 'Make me see de wound.'

He showed me the torn spot in his flesh where he'd been shot. 'A bullet inna dis arm ya right now,' he said.

He explained that the doctors told him that they couldn't remove the bullet because there was a danger of paralysis, which would prevent him from ever again playing the guitar. The bullet would have to stay in his arm for the rest of his life.

He told me about the assassination attempt, how he had been in the kitchen sharing a grapefruit with Don Taylor when gunmen raced up the stairs and burst into the room, their machine-guns blazing. In the confusion that followed, with shots thundering in the small room and bullets whizzing everywhere, he felt a burning across his chest and a stinging in his arm. As quickly as the madness had begun, Nesta said, it passed. The gunmen, their wicked work done, thumped down the stairs and turned their murderous fire on Rita's VW that was pulling out the gate, shattering the back window and grazing her head.

Behind the assassination attempt was politics – at least that was the talk. I don't understand the fullness of it to this day, but Nesta had scheduled a free concert at All Heroes Park in Kingston, which some people resented because they thought it showed his support for Michael Manley's PNP, which was locked in a bitter struggle with Edward Seaga's JLP. The attempt on Nesta's life had taken place the day before the scheduled concert.

But it did not stop Nesta. In spite of the shooting, and even with a bullet lodged in his arm, he still staged the concert as scheduled – two days after the gunmen had tried to kill him. Rita, her head bandaged, appeared on stage and sang right beside him.

After I had assured myself that Nesta was in no danger, I stayed a couple of days and then returned to Delaware. He would have plenty of company during his recuperation at Chris Blackwell's house. Chris himself was not there, but the artist Neville Garrick was, as was Carlton Barrett; and Nesta's cook, as well as some members of the band. Rita was already there, recovering from the graze in her scalp; Cindy was on her way. Nesta was in good hands. I went back to Wilmington and my smaller children.

Nesta's wound would never get better. In fact, over the five short years of life he had left, it would gradually get worse and worse and eventually even affect his guitar playing.

On 11 May 1981, when Nesta passed, the assassin's bullet was still lodged in his flesh.

*

The next trouble to arise during those bitter years of 1976–7 fell on Nesta's right big toe, a part of the body so lowly that one would never think it capable of striking a killing blow.

Nesta returned from Jamaica one day, complaining about a sore toe. He said he had bucked his toe (stubbed it) during a backyard football game and that since then the injury would not heal. He took off his shoes and socks and showed me the toe. Near the nail, it had a small but festering red sore with uneven white edges.

At the time we saw the injury as an annoyance. I treated it with frequent bathings in warm water and by sprinkling it with Golden Seal powder. Nesta himself would also wash the wound and try different medicines on it. But the toe stayed sore and red; the wound just would not heal.

Still, we were all thinking the same thing: that when Massah Death visits the body, he takes up residence not in a humble cultivator's shack of a big toe, but in a big-house organ such as the kidney, liver, or heart. So we weren't too worried about a sore toe.

Nesta and the band resumed touring. They were gone for a few weeks when Nesta called from England with the judgment: he had cancer in his big toe. It was a wicked cancer with a long name – melanoma.

Later, Rita also called and peppered me with questions about Captain that I couldn't answer, saying that Nesta's blood was rare, that it was the white man in his system that had given him cancer. Did Captain have any sickness that I knew about? What was Captain's blood type? How did Captain die?

I didn't know the answers. I told her all I knew about Captain was that he was Captain: I knew nothing else.

It was shortly after Rita's call that Nesta phoned to break the news that the English doctor wanted to cut off his toe. And if the cancer was found to have spread beyond the toe, the doctor wanted to amputate his entire foot.

His voice filled with anguish, he then asked me the unanswerable question. 'Mamma, I never do nobody no evil. I never do nobody no wrong. Why would Jah give me cancer?'

Why?

I did not know why, then or now. In the fullness of time, all the whys of the world will be answered. But for now, we can only ask.

It was the beginning moment of a long tribulation. I had no idea about what to do, what steps I could take to help my son. So I asked the advice of friends and family, and the only glimmer of hope any of them could give me was a man named Bungo.

Bungo was a Jamaican bush doctor, a man who used plants and natural herbs to treat disease and who was said to have cured many sick people the doctors had given up as dead. One day there was a knock on my front door: it was Bungo, a little old Rasta man, sent to my house by a well-meaning friend.

Bungo listened attentively to my story about Nesta and then declared that he thought he could help him.

'Listen me, Bungo,' I told him seriously. 'Dis is no time for experiment. We want to know dat dis is a positive thing, dat you definitely can help. Talk de plain truth: can you cure Nesta?'

Bungo fidgeted and said he couldn't be positive on that; he couldn't in good conscience say that he was 100 per cent sure.

Then Bungo walked through my garden with me and picked some common herbs and weeds, smelled them, and explained their powers and properties. He said many of the common plants we walk on are really medicines. He was a pleasant old man, very dignified and mannerly, and for a while Nesta was keenly interested in my reports of what he had to say.

But after examining Bungo at length, I had to recommend

against him, telling Nesta that for a sickness as serious as cancer, he needed better care.

Nesta returned to Delaware, facing the prospect of surgery.

Nesta did not want his toe cut off. He loved to play football; he loved to dance on the stage when he was performing. He thought he would be able to do none of these things if his toe was amputated. He had returned to Delaware to think over his options for treatment.

Nesta's manager, Don Taylor, highly recommended Dr William Bacon in Miami. He said that Dr Bacon had saved his life after the assassination attempt.

Still Nesta wavered in his mind, uncertain about what to do. Now that it was obvious that Bungo could not help, surgery seemed his only choice. Yet he did not want to lose the toe.

With all this gloom draped over us, one evening when Don Taylor was visiting him, Nesta suddenly said to me in my drawing-room, 'Mamma, now dat Mr Booker gone, you have fe sell out dem place you have and move from here.'

'Move from here to where?'

'Go Miami, Mamma. Now dat Mr Booker pass, you can't manage with all de snow. If anybody a walk on de sidewalk and fall down, you know, a you have fe pay fe dem.'

A little later Don Taylor came over and urged me to do as Nesta suggested and move to Miami. I perked up. Miami was not only close to Jamaica, it had no brutal Delaware winter. I didn't need persuading. If Nesta wanted me to go to Miami, I would go there willingly. Don Taylor said he knew a realtor who could find me a suitable house, and we made arrangements to go to Miami.

For the next few days, Rita and I were up and down Miami, looking for a house while Dr Bacon put Nesta through medical tests.

I saw one house after another, but none was suitable for our family. I had a big family, with three small children – Pearl, Richard and Anthony. Plus there was Nesta, who would be with me when he wasn't on tour or away on business. So the house would have to be big, with many bedrooms.

Using Don Taylor's house as a base, I went around with a realtor named Helena, inspecting one house after another. I saw one here and one there. I looked up and down, back and forth, far and wide. But I found nothing suitable for our extended family.

We ran into instances of racism, too, little pinpricks of bigotry that were annoying. At one big house we went to, for example, the people looked out the window, glimpsed a car full of black people, and came up with some cock-and-bull story about why we could not see the house. Helena was embarrassed but did her best to treat an ugly episode lightly.

We had no success house-hunting, at first. Nothing we saw would do. I returned to Delaware, disheartened.

The next time I came back to Miami, I found a dream house, one that was perfectly suited to my entire family. Actually, Don Taylor found it through word of mouth.

One day we were on our way back from the airport where Nesta, Don Taylor and I had gone to meet Gilly, Nesta's personal Ital cook. Nesta was then still convalescing at Don Taylor's house from the operation to remove the cancer on his toe. Skin taken from his bottom had been grafted on to the spot on his toe from which the cancer had been cut off.

On the way back, Nesta asked from the back seat, 'You can't find a house yet?'

Don Taylor suggested that on the way home we could stop and look at the house he'd heard about. The only trouble, Don Taylor said, was that the house was very expensive.

'Expensive?' Nesta snorted scornfully. Then he lapsed into a brooding silence, for his toe was paining him.

It was the perfect house: I knew that immediately once I stepped inside it. I saw my room upstairs; I saw Nesta in the room below, right at the foot of the stairs; I saw my three children in the three bedrooms off a wing that extended beside the indoor swimming-pool.

His toe still in a plaster and throbbing, Nesta stayed in the car while the owner's friend showed me and Don Taylor around the house. That evening Nesta asked me what I thought of it. I told him it was perfect, but I didn't know if he could afford it.

'You like de house, Mamma?' he pressed.

'I say yes. But I don't know if you can afford it.'

'You like it, Mamma?'

'Yes, Nesta. But can you afford it?'

'You better go look at it again and make sure you like it.'

So I went and looked at the house again, this time on an escorted tour by the owner, and I came back and told Nesta I truly liked the house. He sent for Don Taylor and told him to make arrangements for its purchase. I returned to Delaware to pack up and move my family to Miami.

During the intervening weeks I was peppered by telephone calls from Nesta, anxiously asking me when I was coming. I told him I was coming as quickly as I could, but he kept calling and calling, telling me to come quickly, come quickly.

Don Taylor added his calls to Nesta's own. 'You son well want you to come,' he told me urgently one evening. 'When you coming?'

I was getting impatient with all this pestering, and eventually Nesta sent Neville Garrick to Delaware to help me pack and move. From his great haste, I gathered that Nesta just didn't like staying at Don Taylor's house and was anxious to get into his own place with his family.

In fact, this rush that Nesta was in would later nearly cost me the roof over my head. His original plan was to put the house in my name, but he was so eager to close the sale and move that, at Don Taylor's suggestion, he put the house in his name rather than wait for me to arrive and sign the proper papers.

However, a week or so later, I was settled in Miami in the new house that Nesta had bought for me. Nesta moved out from under Don Taylor's roof and into his own new room.

After we'd moved into the new house, Nesta developed an infection in the toe from which the cancer had been cut and had to go back into the hospital for some further testing.

Accompanied by Winnie and Diane, I went to visit him, and we sat around in his room talking. One of his doctors, a lady named Dr Hedgepath, came into the room and gave us her assurance that they'd gotten all the cancer. She said that she didn't think there was any further danger from the toe.

The news left us feeling giddy with joy. Brightened, we chatted merrily with Nesta, whose foot was in plaster.

When we were leaving, all of us went up to Nesta to kiss him goodbye. He took the kisses from his girlfriends and from me, then, glancing up as we were leaving, he asked mischievously, 'But wait. You have to sick before you can get all dem kiss ya?'

We all broke out into a lighthearted laughter which trailed behind us as we left Nesta in his hospital room and trooped down the corridor.

His toe was still occasionally causing him some discomfort. But the medical outlook, so far as we knew, was good. Trouble, the thief I heard outside my window, had slunk away in the night to haunt some other family.

Or so I innocently thought.

Chapter Sixteen

For a few weeks, Nesta hobbled around the house with his foot in plaster, recovering from the surgery. He fell back into his usual routine: he strummed the guitar, wrote his songs quietly in his room, and was up and down as if all was well with him again. Once the plaster was removed, he made no more follow-up visits to Dr Bacon.

Meantime, I was fighting a daily battle to keep the new house clean. It was a big house in an all-white neighborhood. It had some six bedrooms, a huge living-room, dining-room, a rec room, an indoor patio and pool – all very spacious. Plus there was an enormous yard, nearly two acres planted in fruit trees and flowering bushes.

From my days of working as a housekeeper under many different mistresses, I had acquired very picky standards of domestic cleanliness, and taking care of such a large house filled with children quickly became an endless chore.

One day Nesta saw me vacuuming and said, 'Mamma, you think you can manage dis house ya?'

'Yeah, man,' I said confidently. 'How you mean?'

'A 'nuff work in ya, you know, Mamma,' he remarked, glancing around the room I was vacuuming.

'Nesta,' I said sharply, 'I'm a big girl now. I can manage.'

And I went back to cleaning.

But the work was a heavy load, and no matter how I cleaned and cleaned – picking up here, dusting there, tidying this room, cleaning this toilet or that one – I still found myself falling further and further behind.

One day I threw up my hands in despair and said to Nesta, 'Me have to get somebody to help me.'

He smirked. 'Oh? Den you nuh did tell me you're big girl now, you nuh need no help?'

'Yeah,' I sighed, weary from all the cleaning. 'But is a big house, Nesta. It well big.'

So we sent for my grandson Robbie's grandmother in Jamaica and she came over and stayed with me as a live-in housekeeper.

Nesta was once again taking up his usual style of life.

With the plaster removed from his foot, he was walking normally again, doing his music, going to the studio, traveling to Jamaica, making appearances in England. The nail in his right big toe had been removed, but he didn't seem to miss it much.

But he seemed unsettled and restless with the new house.

One day, as he was planning another tour, Nesta called me into his bedroom and closed the door. He looked worried. With his tour coming up, he was reluctant to leave me alone in Miami because he said the city was a godless Babylon full of wicked criminals and gunmen.

'Mamma,' he said quietly, 'I still have a lot of work to do for Jah. You are here and all your people up in Delaware. And you no have nobody down here. You think you'll be able to live here by yourself without family round you?'

'I think I'll be all right,' I said. 'I'm a big girl now. I have to shoulder me responsibilities.'

He stared at me for a long moment.

'Mamma,' he finally said, 'a Jamaica me would like fe see you live.'

'What? Up a Nine Mile?'

'No. You no have fe live in Nine Mile. You could buy a home in Kingston, Ocho Rios, or any place. You don't have fe go back to Nine Mile. Dem have good school in Jamaica de children can go to.'

'Oh.'

'Right now, Mamma,' he said, 'me no want you work. Me want you look over my business, and see dat things go right.'

I nodded. 'Me can do dat.'

'You see dis ya house, Mamma,' he waved his hand at the spaciousness surrounding us, 'you coulda sell dis ya house and use de money to buy three good house in Jamaica.'

'A so? Den tomorrow I'll call de realtor and put de house back 'pon de market.'

And that is what I did even though we had been in the new house for only about three months.

I called Helena, and the rainstorm of turmoil and confusion that followed burst over my poor head.

She brought another realtor with her and said that he could handle the re-sale of the house, declaring flatly that she wanted nothing more to do with any of our business, because, she said, various shenanigans had gone on that made her vexed.

When our neighbor across the street heard that we were selling the house, she eagerly ran over to urge me to work with an agent she knew. In my innocence, I took her offer to help as genuine. It was only later when her son, in a fit of temper, blurted out to us, 'My mother says if it's the last thing she does, she's going to get you out of here!' that I discovered her rotten motive.

Nesta was away on tour, and I was fighting alone against the conspiracies of Babylonians. It was confusion after confusion what with open houses and possible buyers traipsing in and out, poring over my new house, sniffing through the rooms, eyeing the furnishings. I didn't grasp what was happening, and without Nesta to guide me, I was slipping deeper and deeper into drowning water.

A buyer was found, and before I could overstand what was

happening, contracts were being shoved under my nose for me to sign containing all kinds of whys and wherefores. I was in over my head. I resisted signing one contract but was coaxed into signing another.

Meanwhile, my neighbor's agent was planning to move us to a Cuban area known as Tamiami Trial. Bamboozled, I soon found myself in a small house on a canal, living among Cubans who were known to openly dislike black Jamaicans. Compared to the house we'd just given up after only four months, the new place was dingy and bleak and the neighborhood definitely shabbier. But for temporary quarters, it would do until Nesta returned.

Deep in the swamp of confusion, with one house half-sold and another half-bought, I settled down in the new house with the children and awaited Nesta's return from tour. He would know what to do. I wasn't even clear in my own mind whether he really wanted me here or in Jamaica. Nevertheless, I always did his bidding even though I was, and still am, a woman who bows down to no man who walks on two foot. Yet with my son Nesta, I was always obedient: if he wanted me in Jamaica, that is where I would live.

I just had to wait for his return.

Late one night he came to the new house my mongoose neighbor had inveigled me into occupying. Since the hour was so late and he was weary from flying, he merely glanced around at the new surroundings before going to bed.

The next morning Nesta inspected the new house, walking from room to room.

'Where de boys' room de?' he asked.

I showed him. They would have to double up in one room on bunk beds.

'Where my room de?' he asked next.

I showed him the room I was occupying while he was away.

'So where your room?'

'Dis is de same room. When you not here, I'll use it. But when you're here, is yours.'

'No, sah,' Nesta grunted. 'Mamma, it look like me can't make you do my business, you know. How could you make de people carry you come here so?'

'But no through we de 'pon a rush and everything,' I sputtered, 'for you say me must move to Jamaica. And we trying to get outta de place 'cause de buyer want occupy it.'

'Mamma,' he said, 'me nah sell me house, you know.'

'Yes, Nesta, but if de man pay de money, you know, you can't say you nah sell it.'

He called to a man who stayed with me as a watchman while he was away. He ordered the fellow to load his television into his jeep, as he was going back to his old house and abandoning this new one we'd been in for less than a week.

'Pack up,' Nesta said. 'Mamma, we couldn't move you outta dat house come put you inna dis! Me have fe move you outta dis and put you inna dat!' He was looking vexed with me. 'You see dis ya house,' he said, 'dis is a gun house. Dis is directly a gun house. And you see dat canal. Every time rain fall, de water goin' come right up inna de house. Here so is not a good place for you, Mamma.'

So we moved from the little house in Tamiami and back into the dream house that Nesta had bought me. The buyer sued for breach of contract. Nesta contacted Diane Jobson and she counter-sued. Things were batted around from lawyer to lawyer with charges and counter-charges buzzing back and forth, but eventually Diane made the strong point that without a power of attorney from Nesta, I didn't have the authority to sell his property. And soon the whole blabber-blabber died down and we were back in the original house Nesta had bought me when he moved me from Delaware.

I live there still.

*

Nesta and his manager Don Taylor had always had their differences. But the first serious dispute I witnessed between them happened at this very house that Nesta bought me in Miami. It happened because of some money quarrel – I don't know the fullness of it. All I know is that one day Nesta backed up Don Taylor in the drawing-room and gave him a good thump, toppling him over on his backside.

I ran to Nesta and cried, 'No! No! No trouble him. No trouble him.'

Don Taylor scrambled to his feet, brushing himself off, bawling, 'Wha' happen, Bob? Where dis ya come from?' And he rushed after Nesta, babbling explanations.

There was a concert shortly afterwards in Gabon, and a serious dispute between Nesta and Don Taylor developed over some fees that Nesta felt he hadn't been paid that were due to him. I heard later that Nesta gave Don Taylor another chastisement over that.

So things between them were building, and one day Nesta finally decided that he had had it with Don Taylor. He sent for him and when Don Taylor arrived, Nesta and one of his best friends, Skill Cole, escorted him into the back room and closed the door. Yvette was also present. Apparently Nesta's intention on this visit was to cut off his management contract with Don Taylor, and he had some paper that he wanted him to sign to that effect.

I'd paid no attention to Don Taylor's arrival because I had been busy in the kitchen. When he'd walked past, we'd exchanged only the briefest greeting. Over the years, there were many things about the man that I would learn to dislike. One day, for example, I heard him say to his wife, April, 'Come on, ole fowl.'

'How can you call de woman dat?' I challenged him.

He just laughed: he thought it was funny to call his wife and faithful companion 'old fowl' in the presence of other people.

Another time I told Don Taylor I wanted to buy a new car. He asked me what kind of car I had in mind. I said a Cadillac.

'I really don't see Miss Booker driving a Cadillac,' he scoffed.

'Why you say dat?' I asked.

April added, 'Make de lady buy whatever car she want to buy.'

A couple of days later as we were on our way to the airport in Don Taylor's car to pick someone up, I asked him, 'Hey, Don Taylor, what kind a car dis?'

'A Cadillac,' he said cockily.

'Den why you say me shouldn't have one and is one you driving?'

'Me no mean nothing, Mother Booker,' he squealed. 'Me only mean fe say dem car ya big.'

'No care how it big,' I replied. 'Is what me want.' I thought his attitude grudgeful and small-minded.

On this occasion, after Don Taylor and Nesta had disappeared into the back room to do their business, I returned to cooking the meal, leaving them with their affairs. A few minutes later a blood-curdling scream rang from the back of the house. It was Don Taylor bawling, 'Lawd, murder! Murder! Help! Murder!'

I ran to the office, pushed open the door, and barged into the room. Don Taylor was flat on his back, screaming and cowering on the floor, while Nesta stood over him. Evidently, Don Taylor wasn't signing the paper as he was asked to do.

'Mother Booker!' Don Taylor blubbered. 'Mother Booker! Help! Help, Mother Booker!'

'All right, Mamma,' Nesta said smoothly, 'you just go back out dere so. Go on back round so.'

'No trouble him,' I begged. 'No lick him no more.'

Nesta yanked him up off the floor, gave him a violent shake, and threw him towards the door. Don Taylor slunk quickly out of the room and scampered into his car. Then he roared out the driveway like the devil was on his tail.

A few minutes later, Nesta, Skill Cole and Yvette went out together. I returned to cooking dinner.

The doorbell chimed. A white woman was standing at my door, flashing a badge. She introduced herself as Sergeant So-and-so of the State Police.

'May I speak to Robert Marley?' she asked.

'He's not here,' I told her.

Peering into the house, she spotted one of my workmen in the dim light.

'So, who's that?' she asked, pointing.

'Robert Marley is not here,' I said sharply. 'No matter who dat is. Is not Robert Marley.'

She consulted a clipboard. 'What about Yvette Anderson?'

'She's not here, either.'

'And Alan Cole?'

'None of dem here.'

She handed me a card and told me that as soon as any of the three returned they were to call her, that a formal complaint had been filed against them for assault. Then she got in her unmarked car and drove away.

A few minutes later, Nesta, Skill Cole and Yvette returned and I told them breathlessly that the police had just been here asking for them.

'Don Taylor send police here?' Nesta asked with scorn. 'I knew he would do dat.'

Nesta got on the phone with Danny Sims, one of his early producers, and told him that Don Taylor had sent police round to his yard.

'Take care o' it fe me, nuh,' I heard Nesta say.

Danny said he would. And he did, for nothing more came of the incident. The police never returned, and no charges were ever filed.

Personally, I always thought my son was far too lenient with Don Taylor. Nesta was not a hard man to deal with. As far as

I'm concerned, whatever chastisement he gave to Don Taylor was richly deserved.

Judgment Day came for Nesta not long after his last chastisement of Don Taylor. And it fell on the whole family as unexpectedly as a clap of thunder on a cloudless day.

One day the phone rang: it was Rita calling from New York to say that Nesta was sick. But she did not tell me the story to the fullest, only that Nesta was not feeling well.

Shortly afterwards, the phone rang again and Yvette answered. She huddled in a corner, whispering in the mouthpiece, looking stricken with worry. When she hung up I asked her bluntly, 'What's going on?'

'I don't know,' she said, trying to sound offhand. 'Bob's very sick, but I'm not sure what's happening. They'll call back and let you know.'

I knew right away that everyone was trying to hide something from me: I could smell trouble in the breeze. They'd done this to me before, even though I'd repeatedly urged them to always be open and above board with me so I could bring prayer to bear on any tribulation. But because they knew I had high blood pressure, they always tried to hide any trouble or worries from me.

From the way everyone was whispering around me or murmuring into the telephone, I knew something serious was going on. Stories began appearing in the news that Nesta had collapsed in Central Park in New York while jogging.

When Nesta came home a few days later, he looked tired and drawn. I asked him what had happened and he said his head had suddenly started to spin and he'd passed out in the park.

I asked him the usual mother's questions: had he gotten enough sleep the night before? Could he have been hungry? Did someone give him some strange food or drink? What did the doctor say?

He said he had to return to New York for more tests. Don't worry youself, Mamma, he said. He would be all right.

But the sneaky whispering; the guarded looks I was getting when I entered a room; the sudden silence that fell among talkers once I came within earshot; the gloominess that seemed to surround Nesta on this brief visit: all these signs told me that something bad was in the breeze, something no one wanted me to hear.

'Listen!' I said to any who would heed. 'If me don't know now, me goin' know later. So better me know now when me can pray and ask Jah for guidance and support.'

'Know what?'

'Nothing to know.'

'Who say anything wrong?'

'Ask your son, nuh.'

'Everything under control, Mother Booker.'

'Me no know wa' you a talk 'bout.'

And so it went for those few days that Nesta returned home after collapsing in Central Park. Soon he left again for New York, for further medical tests, he said, acting cool and calm about it.

He would never again return to my house.

A few days after Nesta was gone, I received an urgent call from New York: come quickly; your son needs you. He was staying in New York, at an apartment owned by a friend.

I hurried to his side and got a dose of bitter news: Nesta had a brain tumor. The cancer had traveled from his toe to his brain. It was inoperable and untreatable. The doctors said they could do no more. They had sent him home to die.

They said Nesta had, at the most, three weeks to live.

In New York, I stayed with Nesta for three nights. We prayed together for strength; I read him the Bible, especially his favorite passages. We shared many quiet moments together, but we did not discuss death or what the doctors had said. Nesta said that

Danny Sims had advised him to make a will. But Nesta was stubborn; he hadn't given up on life.

'Den no when man ready fe dead dat him make will?' he asked scornfully. 'Who ready fe dead?'

He'd sent to Jamaica for Dr Carl Fraser (Pee Wee), a Rasta brother who was a medical doctor at the University of the West Indies Hospital. Pee Wee arrived to be with him during the medical consultations. After going over Nesta's charts and consulting with the New York doctors, Pee Wee had come up with a last-resort idea: Nesta would travel to Germany and be treated at the clinic of Dr Josef Issels in Bavaria.

Chapter Seventeen

When I think back to the way Nesta was before the doctors gave him a death sentence, I feel sure now that he hid from us the terrible pain he was suffering. I remember, for example, one time during a concert performance of 'Exodus' when Nesta was singing, that he suddenly bent over and grabbed his head, as if it was paining him. Later, in Germany, I would see him torn to pieces by headaches so wicked they made him cry like a baby. But not for nothing was Nesta's nickname 'Tuff Gong'. Even facing death, he fought a hard fight to the bitter end.

Nesta left for Germany in October 1980. I stayed behind in Miami with my small children. For the first few weeks I heard regularly from Nesta about his treatment and how he was progressing at Dr Issels' clinic.

I didn't know anything about Dr Issels. Nesta had gone to him on the recommendation of Pee Wee, who said Issels had worked miracles with patients other doctors had given up for dead. I didn't even know where Pee Wee got this information from; none of us knew. But since Pee Wee was a brother Rasta and a doctor, we trusted his judgment.

In any case, Issels was our last hope. The New York doctors had given up on Nesta, telling him that further treatment would be of no use. Pee Wee had also mentioned a clinic in Mexico that Steve McQueen, the actor, had gone to for treatment. But Steve McQueen had died from his cancer. Issels seemed to be our only chance.

With Nesta in Germany were a group of his friends: Skill Cole; Bird, a Trench Town brother who had the reputation in Jamaica of being a gunman and who had gone along as Nesta's cook – Nesta had apparently met Bird at Danny Sims's apartment in New York; Wolfgang, a German friend of Nesta's, was sometimes with him as a translator; Denise Mills, Chris Blackwell's right-hand woman, who has since passed on, would also come and go. Rita came once or twice, but mostly stayed in Jamaica. Diane Jobson, Nesta's lawyer and best friend, was there on and off most of the time.

Pascalene, the daughter of the President of Gabon, would sometimes be there, along with her sister. They would stay in a nearby hotel and visit Nesta daily at the rented house. As Nesta grew weaker and weaker, Pascalene would often come over to the house early in the morning to dress him for his daily visits to the clinic where he would receive treatment.

I made three visits to be with Nesta during the six months in Germany. We rented a total of three houses over those dreadful weeks and months, moving from one to the other as the short-term rentals expired. With every visit, I found him smaller, frailer, thinner. As the months of dying dragged past, the suffering was etched all over his face. He would fall into fits of shaking, when he would lose all control and shiver from head to toe like a coconut leaf in a breeze. His eyes would turn in his head, rolling in their sockets until even the white jelly was quivering. Bird would then grab him from behind and hold him until the shivering passed.

Everyone in the group agreed that only Bird knew the right way to hold Nesta during these fits. So Bird became Nesta's official holder during his seizures. Not that they happened that often. In fact, I only saw Nesta have two seizures during those months when I stayed with him. Bird held him both times.

When I look back today on those months, I'm sorry that I

didn't do some of the things I was tempted to do during Nesta's last days.

I'm sorry I didn't feed him more. Part of Issels' treatment required putting Nesta on a strict on-and-off diet. For a whole week sometimes Nesta would be allowed no nourishment other than what he got intravenously. Constantly hungry, even starving, he wasted away to a skeleton. To watch my first-born shrivel up to skin and bone ripped at my mother's heart. Moreover, with no solid food in his stomach, Nesta's tripe knotted up and became blocked. Issels had to cut open his belly to clear it.

The other thing I still regret is that I didn't follow my mind and do as I wanted to do many times: box down that Issels.

Nesta had been in Germany only a couple of weeks when he called and asked me to come and stay with him. He was living then in a small three-bedroom house he'd rented from a teacher who was away on holiday. I made arrangements for the care of my smaller children and hurried to his side.

I quickly found myself in a snake-pit of bickering and quarrelsomeness among the hangers-on that surrounded him.

When I arrived at the airport, Wolfgang met me and complained the whole way to the house about Bird, Pee Wee and Skill Cole. It seemed that they resented Wolfgang because Nesta had entrusted him with a bag of money for their daily living expenses. The whole long drive back to the house I heard about their shenanigans. From the start, it was all back-biting, susssussing, jealousy, and conniving among those present at what turned out to be a death-watch.

But I would find out for myself later. For now, on this first visit, all I had to judge were Wolfgang's complaints.

Nesta was glad to see me, and he introduced me to everyone sharing the small rented house with him. Then we sat in the drawing-room and chit-chatted.

His hair had fallen out from the radiation treatment, leaving him completely bald. He was looking thin, haggard and gaunt. He tired easily, his body being full of the poison of cancer added to Issels' medicine.

The rented house was in a countrified part of Germany, a valley with plenty scenic pastureland and bush abounding. Nearby was a lake. Ringing the valley was a row of mountains whose snowy white peaks looked like they wore a dunce cap. The air was fresh and cool, and even during the early fall and late spring months, you needed a blanket at night. Because it was such a rural setting, we often went for walks down the country lanes, cutting across the grassy commons and following footpaths into the forest.

Down the road, not far away, was the Issels clinic, which was a two-story house built against the mountainside. The treatment rooms where Nesta received radiation and whatever else Issels was doing to him were on the second floor. I went with him shortly after I arrived and met Issels, a tall, white-haired, older man – traveling through his seventies – with the gruff manners of a bully who was accustomed to getting his own way in everything.

The daily routine during Nesta's stay in Germany remained the same, even as we moved from one house to the other. Nesta would awake early every morning to travel to the clinic for treatment. He would sometimes be up for five-thirty and leave the house with Pee Wee at six.

In the beginning Nesta would dress himself and shuffle into the kitchen, where he would drink a cup of tea before leaving for the clinic. Later as his cancer gradually got worse and worse, I'd have to help him dress, for he would be so weak he would barely be able to pull on his own pants. He was in constant pain, some days worse than others.

Most of the time, the morning treatment at the clinic would be administered by a nurse, with Pee Wee being the only doctor present. Rarely, if ever, was Issels himself at these treatment sessions. Sometimes Nesta would leave from the clinic and travel to the hospital, where he would receive other hocus-pocus treatments. But usually if he went to the hospital it would be to have water drawn from his lungs, for his heart was breaking down.

One day after such a treatment, Bird returned to the house without Nesta and gave me the white shirt to wash that Nesta had left the house wearing that morning. The shirt was soaked in so much blood that it was caking up stiff like a piece of cardboard, frightening me so much I nearly died. Horrified, I asked Bird, 'What happen to Nesta?'

He laughed. 'A nuh nothing, Modder,' he grinned. He said, with a smirk that the doctors had pushed a wire into Nesta's back to draw water off his lungs, and when they were pulling it out, the end of the wire had hooked into his skin and made him bleed. That was why Nesta was still at the hospital, because he had bled so heavily that morning that he was too weak to return home just now. All this Bird related in an uncaring, jokey-jokey voice, like he thought it was funny.

It took me three full basins to wash off the blood from that shirt. And when I saw the great quantity of blood mixed in the water that morning, I said to myself, 'Jah Rastafari! Dis ya blood couldn't come from somebody who goin' live. It no possible. Something wrong. Something wrong bad.'

After he returned home from his early-morning treatments, usually around eight-thirty or nine, Nesta would go up to his room to nap or watch television. Pascalene had bought him a television, and he spent a lot of time watching it. He especially liked to watch Bruce Lee kung-fu movies.

The rest of the morning he would spend dozing, watching television or reading. He loved to read his Bible quietly to himself, or Diane Jobson or I would take turns reading it to him. If he felt up to it, after lunch – assuming it was a food week – he would go outside and try to take a short walk. Sometimes he would have to go back to the clinic in the late afternoon for another treatment.

During the long days, between spells of reading, napping or watching television, Nesta would sometimes pick up his guitar and try to play it. But by this time the bullet still in his arm had begun to affect the nerves, making him barely able to move his fingers. One time, for example, I remember Al Anderson, a member of the Wailers band, visited Nesta and wrote out some chords of a new song for him to play.

Nesta couldn't play them. He picked up the guitar and tried. But he was only fumbling, his fingers stiff, clumsy, with no feeling in them. He slapped them vainly across the strings but couldn't manage to coax a tune out of the instrument. Eventually he laid down the guitar with a shrug.

Sometimes, as the long days stretched past, especially if the weather was fine, Nesta would feel strong enough to try a little exercise. One time I remember Pee Wee inveigled him to come outside and kick the soccer ball, and Nesta joined in, tapping the ball back and forth across the lawn. But soon breath began to leave him, and he began to pant like he was winded. He went back into the house and, while he sat at the dinner table trying to catch his breath, immediately suffered a seizure. It was one of the two seizures Nesta suffered in Germany that I witnessed. They struck him like an earthquake, making his whole body vibrate from the inside.

Over the months, his head would pain him so much he would lie on the bed, moaning. Sometimes the pain would bring water to his eye. Then when his tripe knotted up, to headache pain was added the terrible affliction of bellyache pain, which is one of the worst pains flesh and blood can suffer. It would drag on so, for one long painful month after the other, and every day would be a knife that death stabbed and twisted anew in an already open, bleeding wound.

*

On my first visit, however, things were not so bleak. I settled down in the house to care for my son, to wash and iron his clothes, tidy up his bedroom, help him get up and move about.

Later, I would have to dress him. Over the months we would share a bedroom together, then a bed. At night I would have to supply him with bedpans because it became too hard for him to get out of bed and walk the few steps to the bathroom. I remember he would often ask me, with amazement, 'How you know me need a bedpan?' And I would reply, 'Me just have de feeling.'

But that would come later as the days got shorter, and the nights longer and darker. For now, he seemed only sick, not on death's doorstep.

On my first visit, Nesta wanted to impress me with how able-bodied he was, how strong and hearty he felt. So that Sunday he said he wanted us to go for a walk through the woods at the foot of the mountains.

We set out on our walk, Nesta racing ahead. Wolfgang pointed out a high mountain peak in the distance and told me, with wonder, that Nesta had climbed it on his own just weeks ago when they had first arrived in Germany. Wolfgang said that he himself had been unable to keep up and hadn't made it to the top.

The day was bright and sunny. It was fall, and there was a nip in the breeze, but with a touch of warmth still lingering in the sun's husk. We hiked through a forest whose trees were either stripped bare or whose few shriveled-up leaves dangled from the branches, making the noise of a hundred baby-rattles in the breeze.

Nesta raced ahead, turning to chatter excitedly over his shoulder at me, as I chugged along like an old, leaky steamroller. He was acting frisky, bounding over roots and stones in a park at the base of the mountain.

'Come, Mamma,' Nesta said, waving to me, 'we have far to go.'

We passed Dr Issels out for a brisk walk with his son, and as he blew past he shouted at Nesta, 'Good, Bobby! The walking is very good for you.'

At the top of the mountain towering over us was the cable car landing built next to a huge iron cross. But before we could start up the trail that crisscrossed the mountainside, we had to cross a wooden pontoon bridge over a dark green pond.

Nesta was nearly across the bridge when his eyes suddenly turned in his head, he stopped dead in his tracks, and began an uncontrollable trembling. Bird, who was trailing close behind him, grabbed him and held him tight, and Nesta continued to shiver and twitch in his grasp, making the two of them shake like one body jolted by an electric shock.

Nesta was clearly winded. We started back towards the house. I suggested that we take what seemed to me to be a short cut through the commons, and soon we were hopelessly lost and out of sight of the main road. Nesta couldn't go on. He sat on a bench by the roadside, while Bird headed back to the house to get the car.

Near where we rested was a woodland shrine to the Virgin Mary, and Nesta and I sat quietly there on the edge of the woods while the evening slowly rolled in on us in a tide of dimness. He glanced up at the top of the mountain and panted, 'Mamma, I wanted to carry you to de top.'

'I reach far enough already.'

Shivering in the evening chill, he was blowing hard from all the walking. His beautiful locks were all gone, his bald head hidden under a tam. He looked pale and haggard.

'I reach it de first time,' he muttered.

'You goin' reach it again. But not today. Me foot can't go no further.'

'You tired?'

'Very tired. Not a step more left in dis old foot today.'

'One day before you leave,' he vowed, 'I'll carry you to dat mountain top.'

Jah Rastafari bless you, son. You tried. You tried as hard as you could. But you and I were never to reach the top of that old German mountain.

We were grasping at straws, during those grim days, trying to find a way, any way, to save Nesta. When I went home, there would be a stack of letters from the fans, offering all manner and kind of remedies for curing cancer. This one would say that such-and-such a relative had been cured by doing so-and-so, and the prescriptions they offered would range from the far-fetched to the ridiculous. That Nesta was dying in Germany was all over the newspapers, and every time an article about his condition appeared in any major publication, a flood of mail would pour into the record company and be forwarded to my house.

I myself was racking my brain, trying to do something, anything. One evening as I sat reading the Bible to Nesta, he moved his injured arm in an awkward way, and I had a sudden inspiration.

'But wait, Nesta!' I cried. 'De bullet nuh still inna your arm?'

He groaned, for his head was paining him, and said yes.

'Dr Issels know?' I asked, getting excited.

'Me nuh believe so.'

'But you should tell him, you know! You never know, maybe is de bullet give you de cancer!'

He said he would tell Issels tomorrow.

And he did. But nothing came of the revelation. The cancer continued to eat away at his brain without mercy.

It was not long after I arrived on that first visit that the group surrounding Nesta – the Skill Cole, the Bird, the Pee Wee – soon began to get on my nerves. It was obvious to me that they resented having me around. It soon came out, in whispers and sly remarks overheard here and there, that for staying with him in Germany they thought Nesta would reward each of them with a Mercedes Benz to take back to Jamaica. They must have sensed my hostility because soon they got their hackles up against me.

I just didn't like their attitude. Nesta was in agony, morning, noon, and night, yet they acted for all the world like he was a whiner and complainer. It is always hard for the well to understand the sick; but for the man without imagination to feel the sufferer's pain is impossible. And these three had no more imagination than riverbed rockstone.

One of the first arguments we had was over food. Nesta was on one of his no-food weeks, Issels allowing him no nourishment but what he got from the saline drip. Diane had sent over a box of food from Jamaica, as she did every week when she was not in Germany. But as soon as the box arrived, it was torn open and gobbled down, leaving almost nothing for Nesta.

I went into Nesta's room and told him that all the food was being eaten, leaving none for him. He looked up and said weakly, 'Tell dem no eat up no more o' Nesta food.' So I went into the kitchen and told them to leave some food for Nesta. I took out a bammy (Jamaican flat bread made from cassava) and baked it for him, adding coconut milk to moisten it. I served it to Nesta and he ate a small piece.

A few minutes later, he doubled over with a fiery bellyache. He lay squirming on the bed, moaning, clutching his stomach. No matter what I did, I couldn't ease his pain. Bellyache had wrapped him like a crushing snake and was squeezing him so hard that sweat beaded up all over his face.

Rushing between the kitchen and bedroom, trying to find some relief – anything, oh, Jah Rastafari, for Nesta! – I overheard one of them chuckling coarsely, 'Yes, Rasta! De man go nyam up de food, and see it a kill him in dere now.' I could only stand in the doorway and stare at them, unable to believe that these wretches who called themselves Nesta's friends could hear his horrible moaning and be so heartless.

The worst of these connivers was the one named Bird, who swaggered around the place trying to impress everyone with his reputation as a gunman, a bad man. He would curse bad words like raindrops can fall during hurricane season. Every second word out of his mouth was another profanity.

I had many conflicts with Bird, some noisy and quarrelsome, others stupid and almost funny, except he was not a man to run a joke with. One evening I was burning incense around the house because I knew Nesta liked the smell. He used to say that incense reminded him of the smell of Africa. Bird barged into the room and raked me up and down with an ugly look.

'What yu a sprinkle?' he growled.

I told him I was burning incense for Nesta.

'Me no like no woman always sprinkle sprinkle 'bout me, you know,' he said. 'You a obeah woman?'

'De only thing me sprinkle, boy, is me lawn in me house in Miami.'

'Is only obeah woman sprinkle-sprinkle all de time. And me notice seh dat you is one a dem sprinkle-sprinkle woman.'

I stared hard at him. He wasn't funning. He was as serious as a judge. I just looked at him like he was a madman and went about my business. But from the way he acted that day, he must have thought that I was working obeah.

Bird was a man who had more bad words in his mouth than gum and teeth combined. When we had our fusses, bad words would fall out of his mouth like droppings from a peel-head back-yard chicken. And he would always be strutting up and down, running off his mouth about how bad he was.

One time Bird was preparing Nesta's food in the kitchen, stand-ing over the stove letting go an endless steam of bad words while Skill Cole stood by, laughing and joking with him. I went up to Skill Cole and confronted him openly.

'Now, Skill,' I said, 'is a long time now I hear dat you and Nesta supposed to be spiritual brothers. Yet you stand here and hear Bird cursing bad words and preparing Nesta's food. Dis man have cancer! How on earth you think de food Bird preparing while cursing with evil thoughts going help Nesta? How you think him going heal from dis food? Every bite dat him take is more cancer you sending down inna him belly.'

I said to Bird, 'Listen, nuh. Right now, I goin' look after my son food. Tonight him not goin' eat de bad word food you cooking. Him goin' eat my food, a modder's food, which is good nourishing food.'

Bird cut his eye at me and sauntered away from the sink with an attitude that said he couldn't stand a bone in my body.

Shortly after that incident, someone told Dr Issels that I had been secretly feeding Nesta. Issels phoned up the house one Sunday and asked to speak to me. I blamed Skill Cole for it, and told him so in his face. But it might have been Bird who was the tell-tale tit.

'Cedella,' Issels barked, 'I understand that you're giving Bob food. You are not the doctor. I am the doctor. You have no right to be giving him food.'

'Dr Issels,' I said, 'I didn't give Bob any food. Who told you dat I give him food?'

'Just mind your own business,' he snapped.

After he'd hung up, I felt every knot in my body from my big toe to the top of my head stand up. I made up my mind to go to the clinic and put that arrogant wretch in his place. I asked Neville Garrick, the Jamaican artist, who was visiting at the time, to go with me.

I headed for the clinic, burning with anger, determined to curse off that stinking wretch. But as soon as I entered the clinic, I glimpsed Nesta in the waiting-room, where he'd come after one of his frequent visits to the hospital. He saw the look of rage in my face and made a gesture for me to keep cool.

So I did. And turning around, I walked back to the house without saying a word to Issels.

But a week later, we had it out.

Rita had come from Jamaica, and one day she and I took Nesta to the clinic for treatment. While Nesta was inside on the radiation table, Dr Issels walked up to me in the hallway and, without even a 'Good morning', said gruffly, 'You gave your son food. And I told you not to give him anything because of the medicine I'm giving him.'

'Dr Issels,' I said, 'I did not give Nesta no food to eat. And you know one thing, sir, I do not like to be accused by anyone.'

'All right,' he growled, 'I'll find out if you did it or not.'

To my amazement, he pointed his finger straight at my face, pressing its tip between my eyes. 'Now,' he said sternly, his fingertip flattened between my eyes, 'look straight into my eye. Did you give your son food to eat?'

'No, Dr Issels,' I barked back, meeting his stare. 'I did not give Nesta any food to eat.'

Meanwhile, Nesta was staring out at me from where he lay on the radiation table, his eyes beseeching me not to haul off and thump down that damn nasty man who dared jook (stick) his finger right between my eyes.

Issels repeated his pointing technique on Rita, who was gaping at the whole scene as if she thought she'd walked into a madhouse. When he was done, Issels turned to me and pronounced judgment: 'You look more guilty than she does.'

'Why you think so?' I asked angrily.

'Because I have a mother. And like you, she would come in and say, "Oh, baby, eat this, it's good for you." You're behaving just like a mother.'

How my fist didn't collide with that man's mouth that day in the hallway of the clinic is due to only one thing: Nesta. Throughout this whole scene, I could see his eyes imploring me to stay calm as he lay on the radiation table while Issels' hellish machine blasted his head with heat.

*

Added to the callousness of the hangers-on who surrounded Nesta as he fought for life was the attitude of Issels. I wasn't present when Nesta first came to Issels, but someone who was there told me that Issels looked Nesta up and down and said, 'I hear that you're one of the most dangerous black men in the world.'

Nesta was at this time completely bald from the chemotherapy he'd received in New York. He looked gaunt and sickly. His natural way with strangers was to be shy and humble, and I can only imagine how this greeting by the doctor he hoped would save his life made him feel.

'But you don't look so dangerous to me,' Issels added, eyeing the pitifully sick figure standing before him.

Knowing that wretch as I now do, I can imagine the scorn he must have put into that look, those hard-hearted words.

I myself witnessed Issels' rough treatment of Nesta. One time I went with Nesta to the clinic, and we settled down in a treatment room. Issels came in and announced to Nesta, 'I'm going to give you a needle.' Then, as he prepared his needle, he said over his shoulder to me, 'Mother, you better go out.'

'No,' I replied, 'I ain't going nowhere.'

Issels shrugged as if he didn't care. He gave me a long hard look, then he went to stand over Nesta, who was lying on the examination table. He rolled over the waist of Nesta's pants, lifted up his shirt, and plunged the needle straight into Nesta's navel right down to the syringe.

Nesta grunted and winced. He could only lie there helplessly, writhing on the table, trying his best to hide his pain.

'Jesus Christ,' I heard myself muttering.

Issels pulled out the needle. Then he left the room with a swish.

'Imagine, Mamma,' Nesta groaned, 'de man push de needle right inna me navel. Right down inna me belly!'

He was nearly in tears. I went and stood at his side and held his hand. And I didn't storm out of that room, collar Issels and box him down in the hallway.

That was what I wanted to do so bad that even today I still feel the craving. But I didn't do it because as time dragged past and Nesta got weaker and weaker, a truth was becoming clear to us: wretch or no wretch, Issels was our last hope.

We had nowhere else to turn.

Chapter Eighteen

With Nesta growing weaker and weaker, we moved from the first rented house into a farmhouse with more spacious accommodations. I began to share a bed with him because lately he had been having trouble controlling his urine. Even though he went every day to the clinic for treatment, he was getting no better, but worse.

We took turns going with him to the clinic. Sometimes I would go with him; sometimes Diane did or Bird or Pee Wee. Day in and day out, over the weeks and months, through rain and gray skies and snow and sleet, every day he was at the clinic at first dawn light. Some days he would be at the clinic in the morning and in the hospital in the afternoon. Then he would come home and spend the rest of the day in bed, groaning.

His head was hurting him. He groaned night. He groaned day. His head. His head. His head. His head. Nothing could slow or stop the pain in his head.

Weary, drawn, haggard, he looked up one day and said to me, 'Mamma, it look like dis thing come to kill me.'

Then his tripe knotted and he had to go to the hospital for an operation to clear it out. One night, as he was recovering from surgery, the metal stand that held the saline drip-lines tipped over and fell across his bed. After that, he was afraid to be in a hospital room alone, so I would stay with him whenever he had to overnight, occupying the bed beside his.

To the pain in his head was now added pain in his belly. He

had no rest, no peace, no respite from the everlasting pain that ate him out day and night, light and dark, rain and shine, it was always the pain, Mamma, the pain, the pain, the pain. It was in his head. It was in his belly. It lashed him with a thousand blows and licks that made him tremble.

I didn't know what to do. I tried everything. I got down on bended knee and prayed for Jah's mercy until kneebone nearly wore out. I made promises; I asked for blessings; I vowed to do good deeds, to be kind to my neighbor, anything, if Jah would only spare my first-born child.

I rubbed his head; I rubbed his belly. I made him juice. I coaxed him to drink it, to take nourishment. One evening I scolded him for not drinking the juice I had squeezed. He turned to Diane and whimpered, 'You see how Mamma go on. When Pearl do anything, you know, she nuh mind, but as me do anything, she vex.'

I looked at Diane. She looked at me. The thought flashed unspoken between us: Nesta was turning into a child again.

Chris Blackwell, the owner of Island Records who had made Nesta rich and famous, flew in from England for a visit, bringing tapes of a new song for Nesta to listen to, and the two of them tried to talk business. Nesta was then in the hospital. Chris took the empty bed in his room, keeping him company overnight.

And he noticed, too, what was happening to Nesta, for I heard Chris mutter one night as he viewed Nesta lying on the bed, shrunken and twisted up with pain, 'It looks like that old saying is true: once a man, twice a child.'

Nesta was dying, but he still hadn't made a will. No one wanted to approach him on the subject, for none of us wanted to face the ugly truth – that the end was near.

I myself felt in a funny, uncomfortable position. Nesta had bought me a lovely house in Miami. He had moved me from Delaware and put me up in the new house at his expense. I was dependent on him for support and upkeep. What little Mr Booker had left behind couldn't support me and the small children in such a wonderful house and neighborhood.

Yet when I returned home to Miami to see to my smaller children, I found that some of our unfriendly neighbors were still making it plain that we, as a black Rasta family, were unwelcome. They would drive past and studiously look away rather than make eye-contact and have to wave or seem openly rude. There were pranks and tricks played on us by neighborhood children – little spiteful acts of vandalism, petty theft, and meanness – that made it clear that we were different and not wanted. A neighborhood child shot my son Anthony with a pellet gun as Anthony played quietly in our own backyard. I stormed over to his father's house and confronted him over what his son had done. The father, a doctor, was apologetic. He washed Anthony's wound and put medicine on it.

But we felt we were not welcome where we were, not wanted. And even if we had been welcome and wanted, we couldn't afford to stay there without help from Nesta, who was dying in Germany, without a will.

One night out of the blue, Nesta, who had been dozing on the bed, suddenly stirred and asked me, 'Mamma, what's a will?'

I told him what I believed a will was: a paper that said who you wanted to leave what material goods to when you passed. He listened and then slumped back down on the bed again and said no more on the subject.

Another time he brought up the subject with Diane Jobson, mumbling something to the effect that he would like her to give him some of the law. But Diane didn't fully understand what he was asking, and Nesta muttered, 'You nuh understand me,' and fell back into his moody silence.

During those days of dying, Nesta's mind would often dart like a bat out of the cave of pain and suffering he was trapped in and fly off to distant times and pain-free places where he had once lived as a strong and healthy man. He would linger in that distant place briefly, fleetingly, before the pain would draw him back again to the torture chamber of the present.

One night, for example, he was lying in the dark, not moving, saying nothing. The house was still. It was a winter night, and the whole of Germany was crusted over with a bitter iciness. Nesta groaned and shifted. Then he asked me quietly, 'Mamma, was my daddy a bad man?'

It caught me by surprise, this question. And it took me back to Nine Miles, to the cool, misty nights when, as a curious young girl, I would sneak up the hillside to sleep in Captain's arms.

'No,' I said carefully. 'You daddy wasn't a bad man. He was just a poor man. And he run into a lot of pressures from his family.'

I tried to tell him about his father; about what a handsome figure he cut riding his horse across the commons up in Nine Miles; about how his own family had disowned him when they found out that he had married a black woman who had borne his child; about how he was a crying man who would burst into tears over every little foolishness; about how he ended up poor and helpless in his old age because of the disinheritance he had suffered over his black wife; but I had trouble finding the right words, we had traveled so far from that distant place and time. Faraway dreams, those things had all happened before the season of sickness and pain. Plus Nesta had stopped listening because the pain was eating him again, making him groan.

One evening as Nesta dozed fitfully, I began to fret about what would happen to me and my children if he should die. How would we manage in our wonderful house? How would I pay the mortgage? How would I support Pearl, Richard and Anthony? Where would clothes, food and shoe money come from?

Nesta stirred and looked around the room. I patted his hand. Suddenly, I felt like singing. I wanted to ask Nesta some questions about what I would do and how I would manage if he should die, but I couldn't. I just couldn't. So instead of the questions, I felt the urge to sing out my heart's burdens just like my mother used to do in Honeylands, her planting grounds. So I began to sing:

> *I know the Lord will make a way for me.*
> *I know the Lord will make a way for me.*
> *If I only live right, trust in him, and do the right,*
> *I know the Lord will make a way for me,*
> *Oh yes, he will.*

Nesta stirred. He said, 'Don't say de Lord will make a way for you. Say Haile Selassie I will make a way for you.'

'Me can't sing it so, Nesta,' I protested. 'Is not so me learn it, you know.' Nevertheless, I tried to sing it the way he wanted.

> *I know Haile Selassie I will make a way for me.*
> *I know Haile Selassie I will make a way for me.*
> *If I only live right, trust in him, and do the right,*
> *I know Haile Selassie I will make a way for me,*
> *Oh yes, he will.*

He smiled. 'How you say you couldn't sing it like dat?'

I fixed his pillow and made him comfortable. He went back to his fitful dozing. I went back to my fretting.

The long, long winter night dragged past.

Why didn't Nesta make a will?

Many have wondered about this. Someone told me that Nesta once said scornfully about the material wealth he would leave behind him, 'Make dem kill demselves over it.'

At first, I think he resisted making a will because his mind was not on death, but on his fight for life. With all his strength he was opposing death. He could not afford to think that he might die.

In fact, every step he took, every move he made was that of a man looking ahead to life, not to death. When he had first arrived in Germany, he had even gone to Munich and picked out a Mercedes Benz, which he arranged to ship down to Jamaica. It was this that had planted the seed in the minds of the others that they, too, would be given Benzes for staying with Nesta. A man who buys an expensive new car is not a man in the mood to make a will. He is looking to life, not to death.

Still, it was evident even to Nesta that he was sinking. His strength was leaving him. The pain was no longer on-and-off, but everlasting, terrible, and constant. He could not help but become downhearted that he, who had everything to live for – youth, accomplishment, fame, wealth – had no life ahead of him. Slowly, he began to lose heart.

But then one day, around his last birthday in 1981, he had a vision. He was napping on the couch in the living-room when, in a vision, His Majesty Haile Selassie I, dressed in a graduation gown and cap, appeared in the doorway of the room. In the vision, through the fog that swirled between waking and sleeping, their eyes locked. Then His Majesty smiled, turned and walked away.

Nesta knew immediately what this vision meant: it meant that he would die. But it was a consoling vision that assured him that death would be his graduation to a higher plane of life, a beginning, not an ending. His Majesty had come bearing a message of comfort and hope.

After his vision, Nesta seemed more at peace. He described the vision to Neville Garrick, who drew a picture of His Majesty in a graduation cap and gown as he had appeared to Nesta.

Still, he made no will. Months would pass after this vision of His Majesty before death would come for him. During those months, Diane Jobson, his lawyer, would be constantly at his side. Yet he made no attempt to make a will.

Looking back now, I think Nesta drew up no will because he felt a conflict. In his heart, he would have wanted to leave everything to me and to Rita. But there were others, too, to whom he owed responsibility: his many mistresses and baby-mothers, his many sons and daughters.

Tormented by constant pain, Nesta must have seen material possessions as fool-fool worldly vanity. Even as a well man, he had never loved the material world, never worshiped money. 'Make dem kill demselves over it' would have truthfully summed up his heart's feelings, even if he never actually said it.

His birthday came and went. He had turned thirty-six. Many visitors, fans, admirers, curiosity-seekers descended on our rented house. Someone sent him a birthday cake shaped like a guitar. Well-wishers flooded the house with cards and telegrams. The phone rang constantly. Close friends posted gifts.

And shortly after this birthday celebration, Prime Minister Eddie Seaga of Jamaica phoned to announce that Nesta had been awarded the Order of Merit by the government, entitling him to be called 'Honorable'.

When he was well Nesta had always scorned the honors of Babylon. Now that he was dying, they mattered to him even less. Of the award he said nonchalantly, 'Dem shoulda do it long time ago.'

We moved into yet another house.

And as if we didn't have enough trouble already, this house turned out to be haunted by a duppy (ghost).

One night a friend from Jamaica named Melakiah was visiting. The house was crowded then, so he had to sleep on the sofa in the living-room. He was fast asleep when a duppy roughly drew him off the sofa and pushed him down on the floor. Bewildered and scared, Melakiah, after turning on the light and making sure that no one was hiding in the room to run a joke on him, settled back down to sleep. He was just dropping off to sleep when the duppy flung him off the sofa again. For the rest of the night he stayed awake with the lights on, jumping at every sound.

We found out that the owner of the house had recently passed. Diane learned this when, strolling the lawns looking for wild-flowers to pick, she came across a gazebo containing a memorial to the owner's life – a bronze molding of his last boots. It was his spirit that roamed the premises.

Nesta, who was always spiritually sensitive, was the next person to sense the duppy. One night when Pascalene was visiting, she knocked on the door of my bedroom and told me that Nesta was calling me. I went immediately to him.

His room was dark and cold. He was huddled under a thick blanket for warmth. He pulled himself up on his elbows and peered suspiciously around the room. 'Mamma,' he asked, 'you have any incense?'

'Me think so,' I answered, wondering why at this late hour he was asking me about incense.

'Mamma, evil spirit in dis room. Him giving me bad dreams. Burn some incense.'

So I turned on the light, got an incense candle, and lit it to drive away the duppy. I sat by Nesta's side until he had settled down, then I trudged wearily back to my own room, for the hour was late and the day had been long and trying.

I lay down on my own bed and fell into a little doze. I was just drifting off when I felt the duppy settling down beside me on my bed. I was asleep but awake. I wanted to talk, but I couldn't talk. I tried to lift my hand to turn on the light, but my hand would not obey me and lift. It was like I was semi-conscious. But even as I lay paralysed, my consciousness was warning me to get up. Get up! Get up! Something was happening! Something wasn't right!

The duppy was trying to pin me down on the bed. With an effort, I forced my hand out of the duppy grip, grabbed hold of the lamp cord and pulled it, flooding the room with bright light. I sat up in bed and looked around the room, seeing nothing but harmless-looking furniture squatting among their stumpy shadows.

Nobody visible was in the room. Yet I felt an unmistakable presence hovering nearby, staring at me. I lit incense candles.

For the rest of the night, I sat up, watchfully, warily.

Things got no better with the crew of hangers-on. They continued to be just as gossipy and seemed so unfeeling – all they seemed to care about was how Nesta's passing might inconvenience them. I would hear background snatches of chattering, which would suddenly grow quiet when I entered the room.

Rita came for a visit and immediately sensed the wasp-buzzing of griping and suss-sussing among the hangers-on. One night she said to me, 'Modder, wouldn't you just love to hear what dem wretches saying?'

'Definitely!' I replied.

She said she had an idea. They tended to gather in the kitchen at dinner-time, when they would run off their mouths, for nothing loosens the tongue of a Jamaican man quicker than a full belly. She had a small tape-recorder, and she said she would plant it where it could pick up all full-belly rantings and ravings.

One evening, as we were headed to visit Nesta at the hospital, Rita hid the tape-recorder as she said she would. Then we left the house.

We returned some hours later to find the recorder shut off because the tape was full. We retreated into a bedroom, closed the door, and played back the tape, which had clearly picked up the dinner-table chatter. What we heard that night made mouth hang open, eye pop out, hair stand up. These men, who were supposed to be Nesta's friends, were running him down and bad-mouthing him. It made me think they cared no more about him than a dog for an old chew-up bone.

We were listening like we had been struck dumb when one of the wretches returned and began pounding on the front door to be let in. Horrified at what we heard on the tape, we just sat on the bed staring, not moving.

'Somebody at de door,' I finally said, as the pounding shook the whole house with its violence.

'Make dem stay deh,' Rita said scornfully.

The pounding continued, and over the racket we could hear a voice screaming bad words. I got up, went to the door, and opened it.

Bird burst into the hallway, his face twisted up to spew the bad words and oaths out of the gutter that was his mouth. He was screaming at the top of his lungs, calling me every breed of word that Jamaicans use to cuss one another.

'You nuh hear me a knock?' he shrieked, his face puffy with fury.

'Who you think you talking to, boy?' I asked him.

He exploded anew with his rat-a-tat of guttersnipe profanities. Just then, Nesta phoned from the hospital. In the background he could hear Bird ranting and raving. He asked what that noise was, and Rita told him Bird was throwing a fit and screaming at me.

'Tell Bird no mess wid me modder, you know,' Nesta warned weakly.

Meanwhile, the argument between me and Bird raged on, with him shrieking like he was about to pop.

'Me hear seh you a gunman,' I told him. 'But me no 'fraid o' no gunman. Just remember dis: de Bible say, he who live by de sword, die by de sword.'

And I left him there in the hallway, shaking with his rage, the first time I ever see a black man face turn purple like a sea grape.

Years later Bird would be killed in a shoot-out in Kingston. His body riddled with bullets, he would die crumpled up on the dirty sidewalk, his blood staining the street gutter.

He would meet this violent death on Marley Road.

Bird, meanwhile, had reluctantly decided that his stay in Germany would not get him a Mercedes Benz, and he announced that he would leave shortly to join a girlfriend. Then he departed, with barely a goodbye. Others followed shortly afterwards. To take Bird's place as Nesta's cook, Pee Wee imported a faisty youth from Jamaica, a boy named Dave. He was so young that on first laying eyes on him, Nesta muttered, 'Dis ya little youth should be in school. How can dey bring dis youth to cook for me? Him can't cook.'

'I don't know,' I replied. 'But me see him have some cookbook a look inna it.'

'No, sah,' Nesta sighed. 'No, sah.'

'Don't worry,' I told him. 'I'm here. I'll cook for you.'

It was obvious to us that this boy was just another mouth looking to feed off a dying man. Dave had been there only a few days when he got into my bad books. I was washing some vegetables at the sink and the boy, who was also working in the kitchen, began to push himself up against me.

I said to him sharply, 'You can't have little respect? You no see me a wash de thing. You can't draw up little more and give me space?'

'Rasta is no respecter of persons,' the youth muttered sullenly.

'Say what?' I jabbed back. 'De Bible tell you, "Thou shall rise up before the hoary head and honor the face of the old man and fear thy God." So if you say you is a Rasta and you have no respect for me, den you have no respect for Rasta, either. After all, you are under dis roof here and is my son paying for it. So if you have no respect for me, den you have to come out.'

Neither Nesta nor Pee Wee was there during this exchange.

They returned as I was busy in the kitchen preparing lunch. The youth ran out to meet the car and was soon in deep, serious conversation with Nesta. I joined them.

'Mamma,' Nesta said, 'what Dave here saying now? What happen?'

'You know,' I said, 'dis young man here don't have any manners. Him come tell me dat Rasta is no respecter of persons. You see right now, Nesta. Is either him leave or me.'

The youth protested that I'd nearly popped the watch off his hand because I'd grabbed him up in the kitchen.

'Jesus Christ!' I cried. 'You can come tell me son such a terrible lie right before me?'

'Yes!' he barked. 'You grab me. You same one come grab me.'

'Hey!' Nesta warned him. 'Don't talk to me modder dat way.'

Pee Wee stood by, glowering, looking vexed. The argument petered out. For the rest of the day, Pee Wee was sulky and moody, obviously siding with the faisty boy. But Nesta's judgment was firm and clear: his mother came first; this rude boy had to go.

After that row, Pee Wee and Dave kept to themselves, not coming down for meals, but driving to nearby restaurants where they would enjoy fine dining at Nesta's expense.

That Sunday, Nesta, who was in the hospital, fell into a horrible pain. He was hurting so bad that he lay in bed groaning. Diane called, begging me to get some pain pills from Pee Wee.

I went upstairs and knocked on the door. No answer. I could hear a radio playing. I knocked louder. No answer. Getting vexed, I opened the door and barged into the room. Pee Wee was in the bathroom.

I explained to Pee Wee that Nesta needed some pain pills, that Dr Issels was away and no one at the hospital could prescribe medication for him. Pee Wee said he had no pills and didn't know where to get any on a Sunday, because the clinic was closed.

Nesta was in agony, I protested. How could he leave him to suffer like a dog?

Muttering that he would try to see what he can do, Pee Wee got in the car and drove away with Dave. For the rest of the day, they were gone, and Nesta suffered. The only relief he got was from an inhalant I borrowed from a neighbor and gave him to sniff. He lay groaning that whole Sunday, groaning without mercy, helpless in his pain.

That night Pee Wee and Dave showed up at Nesta's bedside. Pee Wee said, 'Rasta, me a go make a move, you know, sah.'

The faisty boy stood sullenly in a corner, watching the scene. Nesta looked up at them from his bed of pain and said nothing.

'Nesta,' I said, 'you see who is you friend, right now. Because we send 'way dem faisty friend, dem leaving you, too.'

'Make dem gwan,' Nesta mumbled.

Pee Wee insisted that he was leaving because urgent business in Jamaica required him to go home immediately, that he had been too long away from his family, blah, blah, blum, blum.

They departed that afternoon. With death tiptoeing towards Nesta's bed, all his male friends, his so-called *pasayros* (buddies), had left him.

Chapter Nineteen

There were only women now left behind in the rented house to care for Nesta: me, Diane Jobson and Denise Mills. We had gone from a full house ringing with the chatter, bustle and liveliness of Jamaican men and women to an empty, quiet house with three solitary, mournful women.

During this time of abandonment, Dr Issels was on holiday. Nesta was being treated mainly by resident nurses at the clinic. Pee Wee and the faisty boy had left on Monday.

On the Wednesday of that same week, Dr Issels returned from holiday and came to examine Nesta in the hospital. He stomped into the room without knocking and went to stand over Nesta's bed. I was in a chair, reading. Diane was also present, keeping vigil.

Finally, after rummaging over Nesta and completing his examination, Issels glanced up at me and said bluntly, 'He's not going to live.'

'What?' I cried.

'It suits him to go home,' Issels said calmly. 'He can leave tomorrow.'

I began to cry. Issels glanced stonily at me. 'Dr Issels,' I asked through my tears, 'don't you think it would be wise for a doctor to go with Nesta on de plane?'

'He don't need that,' he said gruffly.

'But is a ten-hour flight. And we'll be up dere in the breeze with nobody to look after him if something happen.'

He stared at me. 'I'll get a nurse to go with you,' he finally said. Then he walked out the room without a backward look.

I went over to the bed where Nesta was huddled, breathing faint little puffs, so shrunken and wasted that he looked more like a child than a man. I held his hand.

'Nesta,' I whispered. 'Dr Issels say you can go home. You want go home?'

He barely opened his eyes and whimpered, 'Yeah. I want go home.'

I went downstairs to make a phone call. Then I collapsed in a chair near the telephone and wept my eyes out. Mrs Issels came by and paused to say she was sorry and ask if there was anything she could do. I told her I felt faint and she patted my hand and said she would bring me some aspirin.

Then she left. That was the last I saw of her.

Most likely she'd run into the white-haired old German brute named Issels upstairs, told him what she intended to do, and he had stopped her with a gruff 'She don't need that.'

We made arrangements to take Nesta home. He'd always been afraid of small planes, so Denise arranged for the charter of a 747 Lufthansa jetliner. Chris Blackwell agreed to pay half the cost of the charter flight, which came to $90,000.

Diane, who was adamant that Nesta would return home in style, went shopping to buy him a new suit, determined that 'her brother', as she always called Nesta, would not appear in public looking like a ragamuffin. We bustled about the rented house, packing, cleaning up, paying off bills, washing clothes, canceling services, gathering keepsakes accumulated over the months, uprooting ourselves for the long journey home. Nesta, meanwhile, remained in the hospital, hovering between life and death, barely conscious of his surroundings.

The next day we dressed him up in his new suit, pulled a felt hat over his head, and set out for the airport. His hair had started growing back and a good sprinkling of fuzz now covered his entire head. Nesta was very proud of the new growth, which Diane had been massaging with vitamin E oil. He was as smart and well dressed as we could make his diseased body look. As he staggered from the bed to the gurney, he was wobbly. Several times it seemed like his breath was leaving him, and he would have to be given oxygen.

We didn't want the media to get hold of the story, so we moved as secretly as we could. Diane was wearing a Bob Marley T-shirt with his picture on it, and when Nesta saw it as we waited in a private room in the airport terminal, he remarked that the shirt would draw attention to who they were. Diane slipped into the bathroom, and came back with the shirt turned inside-out.

But word had spread, if not to the media then to the airport personnel, for even as Nesta lay on the gurney waiting to board the airliner that would take him home, uniformed customs officials and immigration officers would slip into the room, begging for his autograph. Nesta obliged everyone who asked, even though he could hardly write in his wasted condition. Some of the men looked teary-eyed as they saw how sickness and disease had shrunk him into a frail-looking, little old man.

Nesta had always had a lot of German fans, and these men in uniforms who came softly to his side like they were entering a holy place as he lay on the gurney probably remembered him as strong and vibrant, performing on stage with a full head of powerful dreadlocks. They might have even seen him dancing during a concert, flinging his mighty locks around as he sang. Now they saw him looking wrecked and shriveled up, with hardly any breath left in him. Many walked away quickly, wiping tears from their eyes.

No matter what Issels had said, we still didn't feel comfortable flying for ten hours with no doctor at Nesta's side, so Denise and Diane got on the telephone and hastily made the arrangements. Soon we had added not one, but two doctors to our party, and late on Thursday night we boarded the chartered jetliner.

Aboard the jet with the two doctors was the nurse from the Issels clinic who'd mainly taken care of Nesta over his long months of suffering. She was a sympathetic soul who fussed at his side, as she always had, cooing, 'Poor little Bubby. Poor little Bubby.' Now she sat in an entire row of empty seats near the gurney, which was parked in a space near the door and lashed down to the floor of the aircraft. Before she left to return to Germany, she would give me an odd crucifix with only a head on it instead of a whole body. I have it still among my keepsakes. It is a reminder to me of Nesta's crucifixion.

The plane looked strange to my eyes: row upon row of empty seats, no laughing faces, no wriggling children, no weary businessmen doing paperwork, no worried mothers with their babies, just emptiness and a strange stillness, like we were on a movie set instead of in a real plane. There were ten of us in this big, big plane – two doctors, one nurse, three stewardesses, me, Diane and Denise, and Nesta laid out on the gurney, the back of his head to the window. Ahead of us, behind us, around us, beside us, were stacked rows and rows of empty seats.

We took off and climbed into the night sky. The horizon was full of evil-looking black clouds. Every now and again, a serpent's tongue of lightning would spit from the clouds, and the blackness of the heavens would spasm in the flickering light.

I went over to the gurney and held Nesta's hand. He opened his eyes and looked up at me.

'Lightning deh flash,' I told him.

He said, 'I love lightning. I wish I could see it.'

I patted his hand. He drifted off again into the sleep of sickness. I returned to my seat, to think and think and doze. We flew on into the night for hours, dozing, getting up to stretch, checking on Nesta, with the constant roar of the engines always rumbling in our ears.

Nesta stirred. I hurried to his side. He was trying to sit up in the gurney, to loosen his shirt, which was crumpled uncomfortably under him and pressing against his skin. I was afraid to turn him over, so I called to the doctors. They rushed to Nesta's side and, between them, loosened the shirt and made him comfortable. They checked the lines of his saline drip. Then they patted him down and watched while he drifted off again into a deathbed sleep.

The doctors shuffled back to their seats. The three stewardesses stayed in the back, chatting quietly. Occasionally one of them would break loose and wander down the aisle to ask if we needed anything. Then she would glance at Nesta's gurney and drift back to the rear of the aircraft. Diane sat nearby, constantly within sight and touch of Nesta.

We flew on this way, hour after hour, out of sight of earth, sun or moon, wrapped in an endless darkness, drifting in and out of brief bad dreams.

The storm was now miles away behind us. Ahead was darkness and gloom. Behind was darkness and gloom. To the side was darkness and gloom. Inside was the faint, pearly glow of airplane lighting, dim and fuzzy like lint. We might have been locked up in a roaring, riveted metal tomb.

Nesta was coming home.

In the early hours of Saturday morning, around three o'clock, we reached Miami and were immediately set upon by two fallen angels.

They climbed into the aircraft, once it had come to a stop, two cruffy (rough) looking hooligan women dressed in workers' overalls. They weighed about 300 pounds apiece, and which piece of hell they had crawled out of, to this day I don't know. All I know is that they identified themselves as porters and said that they had been sent to remove a gurney from the airplane and to take it to the terminal where an ambulance was waiting.

Then, like a pair of well-oiled demons, they surrounded the gurney on which Nesta lay, breathing nearly his last, and began to manhandle him like he was a barrel of pickles. They rough-housed the gurney down the aisle, slamming it into the backs of the seats, shoving it fast and violently, laughing and joking with one another. When we bawled at them to take care, they looked at us contemptuously and continued their devilish work. Diane flew into a rage. I yelled at them, but it didn't make any difference. In a blink they had propelled Nesta, helpless on the gurney, to the door, and were wrestling him down the steps, bouncing and jostling him without pity or mercy. They pushed him headfirst down the stairs, which cut off his breath and made him feel like he was stifling.

'Mamma, Mamma!' Nesta cried. 'Please don't let dem hurt me! Please don't let dem hurt me!'

The doctors intervened and asked them to be careful. They glanced at the doctors with scorn, barked, 'Forget it!' and continued down the steps with the gurney, battering Nesta up and down like he was a crate of old tires instead of a dying man. The whole way down the steps I could hear Nesta crying, begging me to help him.

Diane, enraged beyond control, chased after them shrieking, cursing them from here to kingdom come, but they just laughed like the whole thing was a big joke, and scooted Nesta across the tarmac towards the waiting ambulance.

When we reached the immigration area, with Diane still raising Cain to any airport official who would listen, we found that Rita had actually tipped the two fallen angels as they unloaded Nesta into the ambulance, sending them back to hell with Nesta's money jingling in their pockets.

The little nurse lady, meanwhile, scurried outside the airport, gathering plants and bulbs and grasses and pine needles, and when she came back, I was shocked to see what a wonderful bouquet she had assembled from roadside scraps.

'I'm taking this home with me as a souvenir,' she said proudly.

We cleared immigration. Now that we were in Miami, Rita was back in control, and she disappeared with Nesta for the hospital.

The nurse rode home with me. I gave her a bed that night. The next day, after the flight crew was rested, she and the doctors would return to Germany in the jetliner. Of all the people at Issels clinic, she was the one who showed Nesta the most love and gave him the most comfort. Giving her a bed for the night was the least I could do after all she herself had done for her 'poor little Bubby'.

We arrived at my house as dawn was breaking. I had all of Nesta's clothes with me, and before I went to bed, I carefully unpacked them and hung them up. I didn't see a bed until daylight hung bright and big over Miami.

That same day, after a restless sleep, I went to see Nesta in the hospital. He was in intensive care, and he knew better than I what that meant. He had been operated on again, to drain water from his lungs, which were filling up as his heart got weaker and weaker. He had a tube stuck in his back to drain off the built-up fluid.

'You see dis place, Mamma,' he whispered. 'You know what dis place is?'

'No,' I replied. 'Me nuh know.'

'Is a place dem carry you when you ready fe dead.'

'No. Not necessarily.'

Just then we heard a piercing sound like a whistle and saw nurses scampering past down the hallway. A few seconds later the whistling stopped, and the nurses filed past our doorway slowly, as if on their way to church.

'You know what dat mean, Mamma?' Nesta said hoarsely. 'It mean someone just dead. Dis is a place of death.'

I didn't believe it. I tried to pooh-pooh his fears. But he was wiser than I. He knew death was coming for him.

The family all gathered protectively at his side. Rita stayed at a nearby hotel with the children. We were like watchmen on alert, guarding our priceless treasure from a prowling thief.

Nesta asked to see his children so he could give them his blessings, and the next day, the Sunday, the children were brought to him, filling the small room that he occupied. A nurse came in, saw the crowd, and said, 'Oh. You need a bigger room.'

And they came and moved him to a bigger room with a sitting-room in the front, and all his children who were then in Miami could come and visit at the same time. He took Richard, Ziggy and Steve on the small bed with him, and nestled them close to his side as he dozed. The bed was so full that Rita, on coming into the room, had asked, 'What dat big boy a do up deh?', meaning my son Richard, who, then fifteen years old, was the oldest of the three.

'Make him stay,' Nesta muttered.

He gave his blessings to the children, hugging them, dozing off as they pressed against his frail, trembling body. To Ziggy he said, 'On your way up, don't let me down.'

The children reacted differently to the sight of their dying father. Cedella was scared and shocked, and hung shyly away from his bed, afraid to approach too near. Some of the boys clambered up on the bed and snuggled next to him. Some were hesitant.

Nesta ordered lamb for them, and they sat and had a last feast while he dozed and occasionally opened his eyes to watch. Family were in and out for the remainder of the day, which Nesta passed between waking and sleeping.

It would be his last full day on earth.

The next morning, Monday, 11 May, the phone rang early. It was Rita.

She said, 'Your son say fe come now.'

I was already awake, meaning to reach the hospital by 6 a.m. anyway, so I hurried around, getting ready. I cooked some liver and blended it to a liquid, for the doctors had said that Nesta was anemic from Issels' fool-fool diet. Liver was supposed to be good for anemia. I also made him some fresh carrot juice. Then I rushed to his bedside.

When I got to the hospital, Diane was with Nesta in the room. She had not left his side the whole night. I gave Nesta a kiss. He took my hand and shook it weakly, and just then I felt a strange and powerful surge run through me, as if Nesta was giving me the strength I needed to get through the terrible times looming ahead.

I stroked his trembling hand and began to cry.

'Don't cry for me, you know,' he said. 'Me all right.'

'I don't mean to cry, Nesta,' I sobbed. 'But I see how you suffering and I just can't help you. I just can't do nothing for you.'

'I'm all right, Mamma,' he said.

'How you feel?' I asked him.

'Feel?' he said weakly. He shrugged and asked me for the bedpan.

I gave it to him. Then I gave him the carrot juice to drink, and he sipped it with a straw, emptying the cup down to the last drop with a loud slurping.

'Dat's a good boy!' I said, rubbing his hand. 'You want more?'

He said no.

A nurse came into the room and checked him, departing with a sad, comforting smile.

'I'm going to take a rest now,' Nesta said, reaching up and pulling the breathing plug out of his nose.

'No, Nesta!' I cried. 'Is to help you breathe.'

I tried to put it back into his nose, but couldn't, so I called the nurse and she fixed the tube and primped him up a bit. Then she left.

'Yeah, Nesta,' I said. 'Dat is better. Now you'll be able to breathe better.'

He closed his eyes and fell asleep, and began a deep, deep breathing. When each breath went down, it went down to a depth so deep that it looked like it would never come back up, but eventually it would struggle up slowly and fitfully from the bottom.

He began to sweat. I got a towel and patted the water-beads off his face. Diane joined me in the patting, and the two of us stood at his bedside, wiping him off, watching him sleep.

With Nesta sleeping, we went and sat in the sitting-room, glancing through the doorway at him every now and again.

The door opened and a doctor entered, a Chinese Jamaican who said he'd worked on Nesta when his toe was first operated on. He asked if he could look in on him, and I said yes.

He went in and came back out shortly, looking shaken. 'He's lost a lot of weight,' he murmured.

'Yes,' I said.

He gave me some medicine. 'When he wakes, give him that,' he said.

A few minutes later Diane went into the room to check on Nesta.

'Miss B, come here.'

I jumped up and went into the room.

'It no look like Bob a breathe,' she said.

'You gwan! How you mean?'

'No. Him no look so. Call de nurse.'

I hollered for the nurse, and she sprinted into the room.

'Check Mr Marley here,' I begged her, 'for it look like him quiet.'

She took his hand, checked his pulse, and said softly, 'He's deceased.'

'No!' Diane cried. 'No! Call de doctor.'

She did, and the doctor came and checked him. 'He's deceased,' he said. 'You have to move the body.'

A few minutes later two porters came and rolled away the body. Rita returned to the room, found Nesta gone, and began to tear herself up with grief and weeping.

But she was too late.

The long, long months of suffering and torment were finally over. Nesta was gone.

Chapter Twenty

There was a funeral for Nesta in Jamaica, a funeral to end all funerals. It was held in the stadium of the National Arena on 21 May 1981. Thousands upon thousands attended, coming and hanging their heads in sorrow to pay their last respects to Nesta. Big shots were there, as were medium-sized shots and little shots, the powerful and the weak standing and sitting shoulder-to-shoulder. The mourners ranged from the then lately elected Prime Minister, Edward Seaga, to the then recently defeated former Prime Minister, Michael Manley, to humble bare-foot vendors who sold roasted peanuts on the dirty streets from whistling pushcarts. They were all there in the National Stadium that day – the vain, the humble, the wicked, the innocent, the cruel, the kind-hearted, the rich, the poor – all mixed-up mixed-up side-by-side in their Sunday best, bowing head for Nesta, crying tears for Nesta, shuffling foot for Nesta, singing hymns for Nesta, murmuring prayers for Nesta, every face lined and creased with woe and sorrow.

Tears fell that day like rain from heaven. Men cried; women cried; gunman cried; bad man cried; good man cried; even children who didn't understand what was happening bowed their heads and cried when they saw tears freely flowing without shame down the face of Mumma, and Grandmumma, and Puppa, and Auntie, and Uncle – all weeping and mourning over the passing of my first-born, my own son Nesta.

Nesta had been eaten up by months of dreadful suffering, but even wasted by cancer and death, he still stood out in distinction. The mortician who prepared his body told Diane that she had never dressed a deceased with such beautiful hands. She said his fingers were long and graceful, and remarked that now she understood how he was able to play such soulful music on the guitar – because of his wonderful hands.

The memorial service was conducted by ministers of the Ethiopian Orthodox Church, but that day, whether the worshipper was Catholic or Protestant, Methodist or Adventist, Christian or Jew, there was just one common mournful feeling uniting all who knelt on bended knee, whether to Jah or to Jesus Christ or to Allah or to Jehovah or to His Majesty Haile Selassie I – Nesta Robert Marley, whose song over the years had gladdened their hearts, had been snatched from their midst in the prime and flower of his green years. In this sadness and grief they came together and wept as one.

I was like there, but not there, like I was in my body, but out of my body and watching from someplace on high. I heard the words but I didn't hear the words. I saw the colors but didn't see the colors. I felt the pain but didn't feel the pain. The day was a blur, a dream, a haze, a vision. I was like one who saw without eyes, heard without ears, spoke without tongue. Oh, Jah Rastafari, that day of grief was the heaviest day of my life.

Later I would groan under a second day as heavy and terrible, although that would be the pain of a later time, a different day. But the day I buried Nesta was a cruel day, and even now I bend under the weight of its terrible memory.

That day I also met people I hadn't seen for years as long-time friends and acquaintances came trooping up to me, crying, 'Auntie Ciddy! Auntie Ciddy!' paying respects and expressing sorrow. The atmosphere was sad but festive and glittery, with everyone chatty and jumpy like they were at a jubilee.

The line of mourners stretched all the way from Kingston to Nine Miles, and every country road and winding lane was crammed with people straining to catch a last glimpse of Nesta. People clung to tree, to bush, to rockstone, to rooftop, scratching and craning neck to see the procession winding slowly down the narrow country roads, the hearse brushing against roadside bush, traveling through familiar fields and mountain lands where Nesta had skylarked as a boy and walked as a man.

Untold thousands clung to the hillside to watch the entombment. They crammed the brow of a straggly hill – the same hill on which Nesta had told Diane that one day he intended to build a house – to watch his mortal remains sealed up in the tomb.

That day was a spectacle, a wonder. The police sergeant who came down the hillside to escort me to the site of Nesta's final resting place murmured to me as he elbowed our way through the pressing crowd, 'I never behold anything like dis in my whole life.'

That day, I sang a song at Nesta's funeral. I did it to soothe Nesta, who used to love to hear me sing hymns. As I sang, I knew that I was giving his spirit comfort:

> Hail to the Lord's anointed,
> Great David's greater son,
> Hail to the time appointed,
> The work has just begun.

When this most grievous, this longest day in my life, eventually and thankfully ended, Nesta had been laid to rest.

But his body wasn't even cold in the tomb before the scavenging began over his worldly goods.

It began with a meeting in the offices of George Desnoes, a Kingston lawyer. There were about nine people who met that morning. Chris Blackwell was present, as were Don Taylor, Rita, and Louis Byles – a banker and the administrator of the estate – plus a donkey-hamper full of lawyers.

The meeting began with George Desnoes reading a statute of

their dirty Babylonian law to me. He read it carefully, from start to finish, cracking big words in his mouth like he was chewing peanuts. He said that Nesta had died intestate, and by the dirty law, everything he'd left on this earth would go to his lawful wife and his children. The mother's portion was a puff of breeze – nothing.

I looked around the room. I said unto them, 'All you people gather here this morning, discussing land and money, if it wasn't for me, de modder, none of you would be even here. Not a one.'

There was an uncomfortable silence in the room. They all glanced at each other. Eyebrow knitted up and mouth showed purse-string.

'All right, Mom,' Rita said bravely, 'whatever I get, I will give you fifty-fifty.'

Yet I looked at the assembled parties, all of whom wanted something from Nesta, who would eat food gained from Nesta's talents, who would buy house and motorcar from money my son had earned by the sweat of his brow, and I scorned them all, for before my eyes they seemed small and pettifogging.

What they were telling me was that I, the rightful mother who had given life to the man whose talents and earnings were now filling their bellies, didn't belong in this room with them, that I might as well leave right now.

And I did leave.

But I left them with the bitter taste of shame in their mouths. For after I arrived back in Miami, I got a letter from the administrators saying that I was to be allowed maintenance of $3000 per month from the estate.

After that first meeting I was kept in the dark. I would occasionally call Rita to ask her what was going on, and she would say harshly, 'Like what? Nothing a go on.'

Nobody was telling me anything. But as I told Rita, the time will come when I will know all, when all will be fully revealed to me.

Things went on.

Sometimes I would phone Rita and she would talk hard to me, like she was quarreling. Soon the children began to get the idea that I was being greedy and troublesome.

Nobody called me. In the scavenging over Nesta's estate, family feeling had been forgotten. I tried to show the children the best of face so they would understand that I bore no one any malice and felt nothing but love for Nesta's seed. But there was a definite distinction going on in the family, and togetherness had gone out the window. Everybody was going on like in a high ranking, while the poor mother who was not high society, who had nothing to mark her identity, was just pushed off to one side and left to rot.

The news-carriers went to work on what little family feeling was left like John Crow nyaming up a dead mule on the roadside. They spread lies and rumors about me to build up strife and stir up bad feelings. People would come to my doorstep, spreading gossip about Rita, saying what and what she was doing with Nesta's money.

I would tell them, 'Listen, get outta me yard. Don't come in here and talk about Rita like dat. Don't come in here and call Rita's name to me ears, for I'm sure she don't know you.'

During this time of tribulation, I got down on bended knee every night and prayed for my family. For I love nothing more on this earth than my family, who are the whole of the blessing that Jah has given me.

But I knew that the devil would be out there fighting to build up bitterness and malice and envy, for these are Satan's tools, his nasty stock-in-trade he uses to peddle his wickedness door to door. During this time of whispering bitterness, I remained in the house that Nesta had bought me, locked away like I was in prison.

One day I got a letter in the mail from Louis Byles, the administrator of the estate, saying that, because of some shenanigans involving the estate, my maintenance allowance of $3000 per month would be cut off. I was now without any means of support.

But when man closes a door in my life, Jah opens a window. When man blocks a road in my path, Jah shows a shortcut. If the mountain pass is sealed off to me, Jah shows me the road through the valley. If the river before me is in spate, Jah reveals unto me the stretch of shallow waters where I might cross.

Shortly after I received the news that my supportance was cut off, I got a call from the president of an African country. He was an exalted man in the world and one who loved Nesta's music. He invited me to visit his palace in Africa.

At this president's expense, Diane Jobson and I went to Africa and were guests in his jeweled palace. We met his wife, whom everyone respectfully called 'Madam', and his many children. We were entertained in a dining-room so big that you could play football inside it and still have plenty space left over for sidelines, rowdy spectators and goalposts. To get to the president, we had to go through about fifty different doors and pass what seemed like a hundred armed guards. Then we sat down and ate food fit for a king, or a president.

Then the night before we were due to leave, a bearer entered our room carrying two brown paper bags and handed one to me and one to Diane, saying they were goodbye gifts from the president.

Diane's contained $5000. Mine had $30,000. I was stunned.

When we got back to Miami, the customs official was just as stunned, for when he asked me if I had any money on me, I said yes.

'How much?'

'Thirty thousand dollars.'

'Thirty thousand dollars!? Is that all?'

'I think so.'

'Where did you get the thirty thousand dollars?'

'A friend gave it to me.'

'Why would somebody give you all this money?'

'Because I am a mother.'

'I have a mother, too, but no one gives her that kind of money.'

'You see,' I told him sweetly, 'is not everyone is blessed alike.'

I was just easy with him, poor fellow.

The rigmarole with the estate dragged on. Even the house Nesta had bought me, the very roof over my head, was in danger of being taken away. Byles came and walked through my house. Agents were sent to inspect it. Under the dirty law, the very roof over my head would be removed because the house had been in Nesta's name and was part of his estate.

On one of his visits, Byles told me that he'd spoken to one of the white Marleys who'd told him that when Nesta was poor and struggling he'd once come to him for help. The man said that he'd run Nesta and was now sorry. I remembered that once Nesta had told me about asking one of his white Marley relatives for help in buying a truck, and that the man had said he would have to ask his brother. According to Nesta, he never went back to the white Marley because he didn't need to – shortly afterwards, Nesta had signed a contract with Danny Sims that gave him what he needed.

However, it was the same old story: when help was needed, none was given. And now that it was too late to help, everyone was sorry. Those white Marleys who scorned Nesta while he was alive are now remembered, if at all, only because of their distant kinship to Nesta, their famous black relative. As the world goes about its daily tomfoolery, wrongs are sometimes righted. Cedella, Nesta's daughter, today lives in a home she bought from a white Marley who was hard up. As the Bible says, 'The first shall be last, and the last shall be first.'

However, Byles had not come to my house to chat about old

times. He had another purpose. He, like everyone connected to the estate, clucked with sympathy that Mother Booker would lose her house, the very house her begotten son had intended to be hers for life. But the dirty unfeeling Babylonian law held hard and firm and was the golden calf that Byles and all bowed down to even if in their hearts they knew that it was wrong.

My supportance was gone. The roof over my head was threatened. I would be left penniless and without even a house to shelter my head from rain and heat.

But Jah would not allow it. He never let my cupboard go bare. He would touch a powerful heart and send it running to my side.

One day the telephone rang: it was Chris Blackwell. This was during the height of squabbling over the estate, during the heat of negotiations over the rights to Nesta's music.

When I had first met Chris a long time ago, I took him for just another white man with money. But my judgment would be proved hasty and wrong.

Chris is a man who loves black people. And although he is a money man, money does not rule his mentality.

So the phone rang, and it was Chris.

'Miss B,' he said, 'this is Chris.'

'Hi, Chris,' I said.

'How are you?'

'I'm fine. How you?'

'Miss B, I hear you're passing remarks about me.'

'Me? No, Chris. I never pass any remarks about you. De only person I pass remarks about is Mr Byles 'cause he's de one who comes into our affairs and don't know nothing about us and putting me down. Him is de one I'm talking about. I never say anything bad about you, Chris. You know de value of Nesta's estate, and I don't blame you for wanting to buy it. But remember what Nesta said. We can neither be bought nor sold. Right now dey not giving me anything. I have nothing. Nothing.'

Chris listened carefully.

'Chris,' I said, 'I want you to help me.'

'You know, Miss B,' he said, 'they can't do that. They have to find a way for you to get support from the estate.'

'Chris,' I said, 'don't even talk about de estate now. Just give me a money out of you own pocket to help me now. A dat me want.'

He said something I didn't understand.

'Wha' you say, Chris?' I asked. 'Me hear you like you a grumble.'

'No,' he said. 'I'm just thinking how the estate can provide for you. Anyway, give me your bank account number. I'll get in touch with Denise and see what I can do.'

What Chris did was restore the $3000 per month support I was getting from the estate. He did this out of his own pocket. It was the first time Chris helped me directly. It would not be the last.

The merry-go-round of scheming and conniving over Nesta's money continued with no let-up or mercy. Tale-tellers and news-carriers buzzed around like mosquitoes and sandflies, sipping lies and blood. It seemed to me as if the lawyers were feasting like wild dogs on the carcass of the estate, eating out so much of its value that soon nothing would be left for the children but scraps of skin and gristle that not even John Crow could pick off dried-up old gully-bone.

The devil sent lawyers for the estate snooping around my house, nosing into my business and private affairs. Lies and gossip spread about me and Rita. It was whispered that Rita had given me $500,000. On the street, people suss-sussed that I was suing Rita. Even Abba, the priest of the Ethiopian Church where I was baptized, came to tell me that I had no right to be suing Rita. When I told him that I was not suing Rita, he said lamely that he had heard I was. I told him he had heard wrong.

One day Byles came up to me and said that he wanted me to have my house but that the grandchildren wanted me out. I told him I didn't believe it, that I would have to hear it out of the mouths of the babes myself, and even then I would not believe it. But they were determined to have my house, even though Byles himself said he believed that Nesta had meant me to have it. Since it was not in my name, however, nothing could be done. The house would have to be sold and the funds distributed among the heirs.

But I knew in my heart that I would not lose my house. I knew that under the canopy of heaven and earth, no one could take this house from me. This house, I told the Babylonians, was given to me by Jah Rastafari. I had visioned this house for months and months, even years, before I first stepped foot into it, and no human hand could remove me from it and it from me.

The administrators sent possible buyers to look over the house, even as I still slept in it. I remember one woman traipsing through my house chattering about where this would go and that would go, writing down notes, making sketches of my house as if they could sell a gift from Jah like it was a tin of bully beef in a Chinyman shop.

One day, while all this conniving was going on, Chris Blackwell phoned up. He had heard that the administrators were trying to evict me from my house. He would not have it. He said he would buy the house and allow me to live in it for the rest of my days.

'Chris,' I said, 'don't you ever talk to me like dat and tell me about death! I'm nobody's slave, and slavery days over. You not going have dis house wid me inna it until me dead, for first to commence wid, me nah dead. If you going help me, de house must be in my name, wholly and solely, nothing half-way.'

Chris went away to consider, for he could tell that I was

speaking with the authority of Jah. Then he came back to me. He proposed that he would buy the house, pay for it fully, and deed it to me. He asked only that if ever I decided to sell it, I would promise to sell it back to him. I agreed. And he did what he had said he would do.

But there is more.

On 18 June 1990 I was felled by open-heart bypass surgery. After I got out of the hospital, Chris called to inquire how I was.

'You have insurance, Miss B?' he asked.

I told him no.

'I will help you out, Miss B,' Chris said. 'Gather up all the hospital and doctor bills and send them to me.'

I did as he asked. The hospital bill alone was $50,000. That didn't include the doctor bills, for when I was in the hospital it seemed that if a doctor even walked into my room, said, 'Morning,' then turned and walked out, I was charged money for the greeting. When I got the doctor bills, they had on them the names of doctors I never even heard of, but I assumed they were the 'morning' doctors who had popped in and out during their daily strolling.

People can chat all they want about Chris. Some of the brethren talk against him, saying that he exploited Nesta, fattening himself and growing rich on Nesta's musical talent. But for me, I always do what Jamaican schoolteachers urge children to do – tell the truth and shame the devil.

I bless Chris Blackwell. There's no man on earth I ever bless as much as that man. He was always at my side when I needed him. And Jah has blessed him a million times, too. Every penny Chris paid for the house or my supportance, he got back from the estate.

Most of all I will always remember that when I was beset upon by enemies, when there was no hand to save or eye to pity, Chris stood right at my side, steadfast and strong.

*

Nesta is passed, but his spirit lingers on around me always, even as it did during those hard days of strife and bitterness. No one dies the way the world thinks, for the spirit is everlasting and imperishable. What is the essence of a man never perishes; it only changes shape and form. It moves through the world, flitting from place to place like a playful breeze.

Nesta was gone and the floolooloops (foolishness) about the estate was still raging. But Nesta was not dead, only changed by death into a spirit. And as a spirit, he appeared unto me twice.

One night Rita was visiting me and lying upstairs on my bedroom floor. That night after Rita left, I was sitting in my rocking-chair, catching a doze, when I felt someone or something suddenly tug sharply on my frock-tail. I opened my eyes and looked on the floor, expecting to see a trickster kneeling in front of the rocker, grinning at his prank.

No one was there. The floor was bare and empty. I turned and looked at the room behind me. It was deserted – nothing around but silent furniture. Then as I turned my head to look again, I glimpsed Nesta, his back to me, walking down a hallway, where he vanished.

When I told Rita about this vision, she said maybe Nesta had wanted her to spend the night with me instead of at a hotel, but I don't think so. I think he just wanted me to know that he was well and still with me.

I visioned him again, this time more spectacularly.

One night I was lying quietly in my bed in the semi-darkness, scanning the room, when I glanced at a big glossy poster of Nesta hanging on the wall. It was like our eyes met, mine as I lay quietly on my bed, Nesta's on the glossy poster.

Suddenly, in the quiet, dimly lit room, the eye on the poster burst open, revealing Nesta's natural eye, staring at me. I could only gape.

'Nesta!' I cried.

The burst eye folded up over his real eye in slow motion like the petals of a flower closing up for the night, and the glossy poster was once again on the wall, a lifeless paper image and likeness.

It was Nesta telling me that he was here, still with me.

He is with me still.

Nesta appeared also to others. He appeared to Don Taylor's wife, April, in a vision one night. She told me that Nesta spoke to her, marveling at the way he could now travel as a spirit.

'What a thing, eh?' Nesta said to April. 'One minute you are here, and the next minute you can be miles and miles away.'

Nesta had found out that as a spirit one second you can be in Miami, and in the blink of an eye, you can soar through the skies swiftly like starlight and find yourself in Jamaica. This is how the psychics say that the spirit travels in the next dimension.

He appeared also to an accountant friend of mine, during the struggle over the estate, and the man contacted me and told me of the vision, where Nesta urged us not to sell the estate.

On the strength of this vision, I contacted a lawyer and, with the help of Pascalene, made an offer on the estate and appealed to the courts to block the sale that Byles was negotiating. The case went to the Privy Council in England which upheld my side. Eventually an arrangement was worked out where the children acquired the estate, through a deal with Chris, and working hand-in-hand, everyone was satisfied.

The lawyers were paid and waddled off with mouth and belly full. My supportance was established and restored. Chris Blackwell was repaid for the help he had given me. A foundation was established to administer the estate with various of the children serving on its board.

Bad feelings blew over and everything settled down again with family feeling more or less restored.

Epilogue

In Nesta's tomb, there was a place set aside for me. Nesta occupies the top half of the tomb. When Jah called me, I thought I would take my own rest in the bottom half. So would Nesta and I lie, the mortal remains of mother and son bound up in concrete while our spirits roamed over the earth, free like the breeze.

But Jah had other plans. The other half of the tomb is now full. In it lies Anthony, my son with Mr Booker, my last-born child.

Anthony was only nineteen when he was killed.

His death began with a white cow that crossed the road in front of a car that Diane Jobson was driving with me and Anthony in it. From the time the cow crossed our path on the narrow country road that runs from Nine Miles to Kingston, Anthony went through a change in personality. It was like his true spirit went away and never came back.

Anthony had vacationed for five weeks in Nine Miles following his graduation from high school, and we were on our way home when the white cow with a hump on its back crossed the road. After we passed the cow, Diane began to talk about how when she was a child, cows used to chase her in the countryside.

'Stop talking like that, Diane!' Anthony said sharply. Then he said he wanted to drive. Diane turned the wheel over to him, and Anthony drove until we reached Linstead, when the car suddenly started to vibrate. I cried out to Anthony to pull over and stop, which he did, and when I asked him what had happened, he said, 'My head feels weird.'

He became fretful and nervous. He asked me for a Bible and began reading it. He began to insist that he was a big man now, and that when he returned to Miami, he would get his own apartment. He asked me if I knew that people were trying to kill me. He began to behave funny.

That night Anthony couldn't sleep. He was restless and complaining about red ants in his room. The next day he insisted that he wanted to leave immediately for Miami, even though we were booked to go back later that week.

We took him to the airport. It was late, and when Anthony found that the last flight had gone, he said he would wait all night at the airport for the first flight out the next morning. We tried to argue with him, but he was stubborn. Eventually, he relented and came back home with us.

The next day he boarded the flight. I was supposed to leave on a later flight, but I decided that I might as well go home with him. Suddenly, after we were seated and waiting for the plane to move, Anthony refused to fly home with me, muttering that he was a big man, and he abruptly got up and stalked off the plane. I ran after him and begged him to return. But the immigration official refused to let us back on board.

'Something is wrong with him,' he said. 'The only way he can reboard the plane is with a doctor's certificate.'

We made our way back to Kingston and took Anthony to a doctor, who said he was suffering from anxiety and gave him some pills, which he refused to take. Eventually, after much confusion and worry, we got to Miami, where Anthony asked if he could take a room we used as an office for his own. He proceeded to move the furniture out of the room and clean it vigorously.

'Mamma,' he said to me, as he passed me in the kitchen, 'please forgive me for everything I did in Jamaica. I love you.'

'Anthony,' I told him, 'I love you, too. And I know dat was not you in Jamaica.'

But then he locked himself up in the room with five bottles of water, playing Nesta's music loud and refusing all our pleas to come out.

His girlfriend, Malena, came to visit him. Her mother had always objected to her friendship with Anthony and had tried hard to break them up.

That morning, I was glad to see Malena because I thought that maybe she could help calm Anthony down. I was thinking that maybe Anthony had been given some bad drugs up in Nine Miles. I was praying and hoping that they would wear off and he would come back to us.

Anthony let Malena into his room. They were quiet for a while. When she came out, Malena was trembling. 'What happen to Anthony?' she asked me, crying. She said that Anthony was in the room dressed in white clothes and jumping up and down, that when he held her, he had been very rough. She was sobbing when she told this story.

Malena stayed as long as she could, pleading with Anthony, weeping over the change that had come over him. When another friend tried to talk to him through the door, he screamed at her, 'Don't come near this door! Fire is behind the door. Don't come near it!'

Finding out that Anthony had a gun in the room, I phoned Abba, the Ethiopian priest, and frantically asked him what to do. 'Just pray,' Abba urged me. 'Get down on your knees and pray with all your heart. Pray like you never pray before.' Abba also suggested that we wait until Anthony came out of the room to use the bathroom and try to sneak the gun away from him. But Anthony never came out. Later, when we finally got into the room, we found that Anthony had been urinating in a bottle, that he had scribbled verses from the Book of Revelations all over the wall.

However, I did as Abba suggested. I got down on bended knee and prayed ceaselessly, without break or pause or stop. While Anthony remained locked up in his room, I prayed night and day, day and night, begging Jah to give him peace.

Sometime later, the sound of a gunshot exploded behind Anthony's closed door. We ran to the door and pounded on it, crying for Anthony. He screamed that he was fine, to leave him alone.

But he was not fine. We didn't know what to do. I kept hoping that the spell would pass, that Jah would restore my youngest child to his senses.

But the spell did not pass. Anthony stayed locked up in his room. No one could reach him. He played loud music. He stayed holed up for days.

When he came out, he had a gun in a holster dangling from his shoulder. He got into the jeep and sped away. It was a Sunday evening. That night he was shot and killed by an off-duty policeman in the Cutler Ridge Mall.

We took Anthony back to Jamaica, busted Nesta's tomb, and laid him to rest under his brother. As we worked on busting open the tomb under the supervision of health inspectors, a small plane circled slowly overhead, making Abba nervous.

The plane contained Chris Blackwell.

At an inquest into the shooting, the policeman was found to have been justified in taking Anthony's life. No drugs were found in Anthony's blood to explain his sudden change in personality. The only thing the coroner found was that at his death, Anthony had been dehydrated.

The policeman's son, then a child of about seven, after witnessing his father shoot Anthony, said that he no longer wanted to become a policeman. He now wanted to become a veterinarian.

Nor did it quite end there, for this is Babylon with its funny ways.

Some years later, I was in a hotel in New York, attending a function honoring Nesta. Weary after a long day, I slumped in a chair and turned on the television. I scanned the stations and came upon one of those police-story re-enactment shows that are now so popular.

This one re-enacted the shooting of the brother of a famous reggae star. It told the ugly tale of Anthony's death. In Babylon, between commercials for dog food and deodorant, a mother can watch her own son shot down on television.

Since Nesta's passing, all honor and glory have been showered on his name. His records continue to dominate the reggae charts. Books have been written about his life. He was installed in the Rock and Roll Hall of Fame. Jamaica has minted coins to commemorate his fiftieth birthday. His birthday every year is cause for celebration.

For Anthony, there will be no books, no records, no acclaim, no fame or glory. But in the heart of this mother, both sons will ever be memorialized in the same niche of tenderness, there, both sons – the famous and the unknown – will always be treasured and loved equally.

Nesta is gone but not gone. His song lives on in many hearts. His music is played and heard every day in some near and far corner of the earth. He was a messenger of Jah, who used a pulpit of music to preach Jah's message. The message Nesta preached was a simple but everlasting one: Haile Selassie I is earth's rightful ruler; peace and love should reign over every race, creed, tribe, nation, dominion, and power. When Nesta had finished spreading the word, he was called back to Jah's bosom. It could not have been otherwise.

Indeed, every moment in life cannot be other than it is, even if we do not grasp the fullness of Jah's reasoning at the time. Everything that has happened to me – every joy, woe or petty thing – I take directly as it comes, telling myself, 'This is Jah's plan. This may not be to my liking, but it cannot be otherwise.' And I accept the good, bad and indifferent with the same faith and trust. Jah is the father, I am the child. Jah is knowing, I am unknowing. What I do know is that Jah never gives a heart a heavier load than it can bear. Never.

Beyond his message, which rings still throughout the world, Nesta lives: he lives and thrives like the breeze, like moonlight or sunlight or starlight. It is only to the godless that death is a fearful finality, an ending of all dreaming.

To those who love and trust in Jah, death is nothing to hold in fear and dread. It is a thing to defy and scorn.

Since my two sons have been taken from me, one heralded throughout the world, the other a mere child cut down before his rightful time, I have seen them both. Nesta had pulled my frock mischievously. When I was in the hospital recovering from open-heart surgery, Anthony came and lay beside me in bed.

You can go up to Nine Miles today and see Nesta's tomb in a mausoleum beside the small house my father had built for us with Captain's money. You can see the small metal bed where he slept beside me on the cool misty mountain nights. You can walk the earth that Nesta walked as boy and man, and breathe the air that Nesta breathed, and feel the tingle of his spirit.

For Nesta is there. He is also in the sky and in the freshening breezes of the mountain country. He is in Jah's warm sunlight.

It is among such of Jah's blessings that you will find Nesta, with Anthony at his side – my first-born and my last – roaming over the earth like a lightning flash.

Nesta Was a Chosen Child

by Cedella Marley Booker

Here he comes, there he goes,
Gifted, loving, running wild
Nesta was a chosen child
Baby born in island mountain of Nine Miles, St Ann's, Ja.
Wisdom and music he applied to the unity he seeks to create

Nesta was a chosen child
Gifted, loving, running free, his youthful years filled
With trials and tribulations. Jah preparing him to
Carry the message of truth to all nations
Yes, Nesta was a chosen child

As a Rastaman he grew to be . . . singing, chanting Jah words
Of truth, one love, brotherhood and unity
Nesta was a chosen child
He planted his seeds in fertile soil
By the will of Jah the world watches them bloom and blossom
By nature's law

Oh Nesta was such a chosen child
So beautiful, loving, free and kind

Jah blessed my womb that gave his birth
Through me he was born Jah's last prophet on earth
Eternal life is his reward for a job well done by Jah's
Command
Blessed be his seeds blossoming in the sun
Long live Nesta's name Bob Marley
A gift to the world full of love
Yes, Nesta was a chosen child.

The House That Bob Built

by Cedella Marley Booker

In a vision deep divine inspiration pillars of Rasta erected on
    solid foundation,
It was the house Bob built.

With reggae music and prophecy, he told of humanity's destiny.
Stone by stone, his house built so strong, mystical music was
    the mortar mixed
In every song, talking about the house that Bob built.

By Jah's own holy decree he built a house to stand the test of
    time eternally.
Pretenders may come, imitators may go, Bob Marley remains
    the star of the show.

He built a house of recognition for all to see, every walk of life
    knows his work universally
It was the house that Bob built. He turn suffering into an
    ideology, made Rastafari his philosophy.
He turned alienation into an independent spiritual nation, one
    love, one love, the ultimate of creation.

Long, long after Babylon has fallen down, the house Bob built
   will remain on solid ground.
We will sing his song and dance with glee, give praise to Jah,
   Bob built the house for you and me,
Talking about the house that Bob built.

People, don't you know I'm talking about the house that Bob
   built?

Reggae music and mystic life, Rasta in a concrete jungle,
   enduring misery and strife,
Don't matter where you go, wherever you roam,
The house Bob built will welcome you home.

One love, one heart, one destiny, one house.
Rastafari lives.

Index

(BM refers to Bob Marley and CB to Cedella Booker)